HEADV

AN AFRICAN AIR ODYSSEY

IAN RODWELL

HEADWIND
AN AFRICAN AIR ODYSSEY
Ian Rodwell

ISBN 978-1-7398535-0-1

First published by Ian Rodwell 2021
Copyright © Ian Rodwell 2021

Editor: Roger G McDonald (www.rogergmcdonald.com)
Cover design: Sandy McDonald (www.sandymcdonald.com)
Book design and typesetting: Michelle Pirovich
(www.thesqueezebox.com.au)
Printing and binding: CLOC Book Print
(www.clocbookprint.co.uk)

For my lovely, supportive, and long-suffering wife, Trish.

You have stood beside a husband for the past 37 years, and have continually encouraged him to write a history of his early life for the generations of Rodwells to come. Here it is.

Acknowledgments and thanks

A special thank you to my family who encouraged and supported me in the writing of this book.

To Roger for his professionalism and patience in such a meticulous job of refining and editing my story. To Sandy for her support, encouragement, and graphic design expertise, giving the book a heft and presence I never expected. To Michelle for her absorbing and timely layouts and type-setting.

And lastly to Grahame for his friendship over the years, and his humbling foreword.

Contents

Foreword

This book tells a fascinating story of a little-known aspect of the Rhodesian sanctions busting effort. It shines a focused light on the workings of Jack Malloch's operation from an insider's point of view. Jack was often referred to as a 'gentleman pirate of the African skies'. Ian was an important member of his diverse crew.

Without the efforts of pilots like Ian, those who conducted the Rhodesian war effort would have found it much harder to continue, making Ian's story all the more worth reading.

This, however, is not the complete narrative. In *Headwind,* Ian reveals his two parallel lives—one with Jack and the other in the Rhodesian Air Force. In this graphic account of his role in the RhAF piloting the DC-3s of 3 Squadron, Ian covers many of the duties, operations, and dangers his squadron faced daily. He laces the tale of his flying life with 3 Squadron with candour and humour.

The army and the air force relished an easy comradeship but also a polished, professional relationship. We certainly valued the work the Blues got through and how much they contributed.

A unique, personal tale told with searing honesty, Ian gives us a vivid idea of those frenetic days where ordinary people did extraordinary things, often at great cost to their personal lives.

Major (Rtd) Grahame Wilson
Former and final Commanding Officer
C Squadron SAS Rhodesia
Johannesburg, November 2021

Preface

Capturing a life in two cultures that no longer exist poses a challenge to any autobiographer. The magnitude of the task multiplies when the reasons for their disappearance lie steeped in race, power, and politics. The planet has changed immeasurably over the past seventy years. Nobody then could have imagined how the world as we knew it would evolve, transforming thinking, attitudes, and behaviour forever.

I spent my early childhood in the 1950s on a farm in the middle of Africa, in a country then known as Northern Rhodesia, now Zambia. My senior schooling, and the portion of my story this book outlines, largely took place in Rhodesia/Southern Rhodesia, now called Zimbabwe.

I can only tell the story of my young life as it happened. Consequently, I make no apology for language or terms that may today appear politically or socially incorrect. This story contains my memories which, although they have diminished in clarity over the years, I believe remain vivid enough to provide an interesting record. I have tried to present the facts impartially. It is for the today's readers to decide for themselves how they fit into history.

During this period, I was involved in a war and carved a career in an airline that directly contravened international sanctions imposed on Rhodesia. This outfit, Affretair, kept it alive economically by earning foreign currency for Rhodesia to survive despite the British government doing all in its power to close the airline down.

I am determined to not fall into the trap of piggy-backing on others' experiences and stories. The following are accounts in which I was directly involved. I refer to others or their experiences only if the telling amplifies or clarifies my story, or if their experiences were subsequently influential in my life. I met many incomparably brave and professional people during the Rhodesian war, and they have their own stories to tell. Journalist Phillip Knightley took the inspiration for the title of his famous book on war correspondents— *The First Casualty*—from the Greek dramatist, Aeschylus. I was no hero but I did what I could to stem the inescapable demise of a beautiful country and many of its courageous people of all colours and beliefs. What transpired in Rhodesia's downfall, like most accounts of a war, is mostly viewed through the lens of the victor. The truth I witnessed has to a degree been re-written, modified, or forgotten. In this re-telling, I speak only for myself.

Prologue

Towards October—always known as suicide month—the African sun burns brighter and harsher, sucking the moisture from the long grass, once green and supple. Brushing through the undergrowth, the sound of your passage changes from a silky swish to a crisp crackle as the rising temperatures drain energy from all on which the pitiless sun glares.

The waiting starts—tense, anxious, nerves frayed—yearning for the first splashes of rain to give life to the newly-planted maize or tobacco in the parched earth. Rain means survival.

The grass is ripe to burn and wildfires come raging through. All hands fight them with the most rudimentary tools, handheld clumps of brush, mostly ineffective. The work is threatening and dangerous. Livestock have to be moved quickly and often stampedes of wild antelope avoiding the flames charge to sanctuary through our ranks, oblivious to all in their path.

Tempers flare with the incessant, unrelenting heat, arguments fester, and depression overwhelms the faint-hearted.

And then the dust. The flint-dry, sandy soil feeds towering dust devils (whirlwinds) that spiral through the land ripping the flimsy roofs off houses. Cars and trucks on the dirt roads create billowing, earth-stained clouds, turning the road ahead or behind into a dangerous, unguessable mystery.

With so little nourishment, the cattle are walking skeletons, their ribcages prominent as prison bars.

All eyes scan the horizon, anxious for signs of the build-up. At last it appears, the clouds changing their form from modest cumulus to vast cumulonimbus piles with darkening bases varying from intense purple to ochre or chocolate. The air is oppressive, the humidity stifling, and then, with an almost theatrical flourish, the rains arrive. Lightning arcs and sizzles, and thunder rumbles as deep as an orchestra of bass drums. The first raindrops spear into the ground setting off explosions of dust. Above it all, you breathe the loveliest perfume that lives dependent on the land can experience, the smell of rain on dry earth. In no time the flat, empty lands, baked to dust for months, are awash with life-enriching water.

What destiny led us to live in this hostile and unforgiving environment in the middle of the African bush?

CHAPTER ONE

Wars, ancestors, and flying in the family

My father, Bruce, was English, born and raised in Preston, Lancashire. My paternal ancestors were originally blacksmiths, which may explain the broad shoulders common to Rodwell men. A later generation took advantage of higher education to advance into more cerebral occupations. Britain's World War Two war cabinet exempted Bruce's uncle, my grandfather's brother, Ron, a leading accountant of his time, from military service. His task was to help raise funds and keep Britain afloat financially. Bruce's father, Aldwyn Horatio, was also a successful chartered accountant. He was spared active military service in the First World War, and was reluctant to see his son, also destined to join the ranks of accountancy, go off to war. When my father won a scholarship to St Peter's School in York (Guy Fawkes was once a pupil) his future seemed predetermined. World War Two would change all that.

Like many young schoolboys, my father felt an overwhelming need to fight for his country, but my grandfather's wisdom initially prevailed and he was accepted to study at Cambridge. By special arrangement, the university allowed students who could pass their first-year exams in one term to sign up for war service. Assuming they survived and were capable, they could return at the end of hostilities to take up their reserved place. Studying up to 16 hours a day, he achieved the requirement and promptly went off to war.

Ironically, in 1947, having been invalided out of the RAF and de-mobbed in South Africa where he had been recuperating from serious illness, he applied to Cambridge to complete his degree. 'Yes,' they said, 'we have a place for you in 1951 due to the current backlog of students.' He never did return to Cambridge, nor to Britain.

At 18, Bruce enlisted and was accepted as a navigator in the Royal Air Force, to undergo his training in South Africa. He was based initially at Port Elizabeth and this small but significant exposure to Africa stayed with him for the rest of his life. He was then transferred to Palestine to complete his technical qualifications. The day he became fully operational, two significant events occurred. First, the European component of the conflict ended, marked by VE (Victory in Europe) Day. Second, he was diagnosed with tuberculosis. In those days, TB was a dangerous and often fatal disease. He underwent major surgery and luckily survived, though emerging with only one lung. His convalescence took two years as he was moved slowly from the Middle East, ending up in Baragwanath Hospital in Johannesburg, a temporary home to many of the war-wounded and disabled. Soon after, my mother arrived as a resident physician at the same hospital. They met and he was discharged in 1947, thin and emaciated. His military career was over. Or was it? The future would turn another dramatic and almost comic page.

He and my South African mother soon married and as she had only just made her way back from a depressed and economically chall-enged United Kingdom, they felt little enthusiasm to return. My father enrolled at Potchefstroom Agricultural College, a largely Afrikaans institution. Unable to speak a word of the language, he nonetheless managed to take all the main prizes at the end of the course. With accountancy abandoned, he would now embark on a life of farming, beginning with their purchase of a small holding called Sandspruit in the district that is now known as Honeydew, a suburb of greater Johannesburg. They started farming in a small way, growing vegetables and rearing chickens for eggs.

My mother, Patricia Goddard, was born in Pretoria, South Africa, and brought up by her mother who was half Irish (giving rise to Pat's and her offspring's occasionally mercurial tempers) and half English/South African. Her father was a cantankerous old drunk who fought for the British in both the Boer and First World Wars. He won the Military Cross ostensibly for leading a cavalry charge against artillery in which he was shot in the leg, walking with a distinct limp from then on. He deserted my grandmother many years previously, apparently disappearing without a word.

Many years later when my parents were living in Johannesburg, my mother, while waiting for my father to have a haircut, swore that the man in the chair beside him was her father. She approached him and her instinct proved accurate; it was Major Malcolm Goddard, her long-vanished parent. He was at the time going through a difficult phase and was virtually down and out. My parents felt pity for him and took him in.

At the time, much of their house was still under construction, supervised by an old Afrikaner. Gradually the work tailed off and on investigation, my father found that the pile of building sand outside had become a re-enactment of the Battle of Spion Cop. Both my grandfather and the Afrikaner had fought on opposite sides during the Boer War and each day would refight the battle while consuming vast quantities of brandy. Eventually, Grandad had to go since no alcohol was safe in the household and he had discovered where my mother hid her savings which he stole to fund his drinking. After I was born, he stopped seeing us and that was the last we saw of him, although my mother later heard that he had remarried.

Pat, as she was known, was a gifted, intelligent young lady, having won a place to study medicine at the University of Edinburgh. She was among the first women to qualify as a doctor at that esteemed institution. While studying there she met and married her first husband, Barney Aldridge, also a student doctor. Under medical regulations of the time, she registered as a doctor under her maiden name of Patricia Goddard, and was known throughout her professional life as Dr Goddard rather than Rodwell.

As soon as Barney qualified he was drafted to fight in the war, only to be captured during the Japanese invasion of Singapore. Sadly, he was subsequently shot by the Japanese, apparently because all surrounding prisoner of war camps were full. He is memorialised on the Changi War Memorial in Singapore.

My mother had to take a year's break during her medical degree, having produced a son, Anthony (Tony) Aldridge. Once qualified she had no option but to remain in Britain, waiting not only for news of her husband, but working to support her son and lecturing troops, particularly in sexual hygiene. Venereal diseases, especially gonorrhoea and syphilis, incapacitated hundreds of military personnel a day. As an infant, Tony attended a small primary school in Somerset where she had recently settled. Fearful of an imminent German invasion, the parents and teachers decided to move the whole school to South Africa where at least the children would be safe. The two teachers with the schoolchildren sailed from Southampton to Cape Town and then to Paarl in the Cape province. My mother would not see her son again for five years. Tony's father, however, was able to pay him a fleeting visit in transit to Singapore.

The experience of moving to Paarl scarred my brother for life as he had no family to speak of during his formative years. The teachers turned out to be abusive lesbians. They would lock their young charges in their rooms overnight so they would not be disturbed, often opening the doors well after the poor children's desperate need of the toilet meant the inevitable accidents for which they would be severely punished.

My brother was finally reunited with our mother in 1946, but things were never easy for them. By then Tony was nine and my mother was working long hours in her medical career while fostering a new relationship with my father, Bruce Rodwell. She lacked the time that Tony desperately needed and deserved. When I was born in 1948, this new infant absorbed even more of her already scarce attention. Tony was sent off to Jeppe Boys' High School in Johannesburg where the dominant language was Afrikaans, in which he became fluent. It was, however, an unhappy environment and he ran away from school more than once. While there he contracted osteomyelitis and had to endure an horrific operation which involved carving septic bone marrow from an infected thigh bone. He recovered, but the thinner leg was from then on slightly longer than the other.

By the time Tony completed his schooling my parents had moved to Northern Rhodesia where they had bought a farm. Tony came to work on the property awaiting the results of his application to join the Southern Rhodesian Air Force. He helped build the tobacco barns and various construction tasks, but also became our protector from the plentiful wildlife. After a short time at home on the farm, he was accepted for pilot training.

He was trained mainly by ex-wartime RAF instructors who noticed that this young man was a gifted pilot. On completing his training, he decided to move to the UK where opportunities with the Royal Air Force were much greater. Coming highly recommended he moved to England in 1955 and was soon inducted into the RAF, converting onto the Hawker Hunter aircraft. On completion of his conversion course he was transferred to an active operational outfit, 111 Squadron commonly known as Treble One. At that time its primary operational role was to represent the RAF as the nation's aerobatic team. In those days, the RAF chose an individual operational squadron to provide the national aerobatic team. Today, the Red Arrows perform that role exclusively.

In 1957 the aerobatic team consisted of nine black Hawker Hunters and was officially named the Black Arrows after a French journalist referred to them as the *Fleche Noires*. In 1958, under the command of

Squadron Leader Roger Topp, they performed a loop and roll at the Farnborough annual air show with a formation of 22 aircraft, a world record to this day. Tony had the difficult task of flying as one of the two wing men on the edge of the formation.

In 1960 the mantle of the national aerobatic team fell to 92 squadron under the command of Squadron Leader Brian Mercer, an ex 111 Squadron Black Arrows pilot. Tony was transferred as a founder member to the Blue Diamonds as they became known, and arguably the RAF's finest aerobatic team. In 1962 the New Year brought fresh honour to the squadron when its Hunters were selected to represent the RAF at the annual NATO Allied Air Forces Central Europe (AIRCENT) gunnery competition, with the team under the command of the Squadron Commander Brian Mercer. By the end of February, the AIRCENT team had been selected. Places were open for all ace shots of Fighter Command but out of the final team of four, three were from 92 Squadron—the Commanding Officer, Tony, and Pete Van Wyk. The African connection was strong too. Brian Mercer had completed his flying training in Rhodesia and Pete was a South African, so southern Africa was well represented. Training continued in May and the hard work and sacrifice paid off in June when the team triumphed by a comfortable margin, beating the Royal Canadian Air Force (RCAF) into second place. The victory was the sweeter since the RCAF thought they owned the trophy by right, having won it exclusively since its inception four years previously. Tony was the overall individual winner for which he subsequently received a Queen's Commendation, a British military award on a par with a Mention in Dispatches.

RAF pilot competency was assessed annually, and the grades ranged from 'below average' through 'average', 'above average' and finally 'exceptional'. Not that he ever told me, but on reading through his flying logbook I noticed he had—once operationally qualified—been consistently assessed as 'exceptional' throughout his air force flying career. The achievement may have been unique; he was once described by the Air Marshal Commander-in-Chief of Fighter Command as currently their best operational pilot.

CHAPTER TWO

Early life in the African bush

My parents married in 1947 and I was born in September 1948. After the war, life was tough for any young couple starting afresh. My father was studying at Potchefstroom Agricultural College, my brother was at school, and the only person able to earn a full time salary was my mother who had to return to work almost immediately after I was born. As a result my daily care was undertaken by Rachel and Gracie, who both came from Basutoland. People of the Basuto nation (today known as Lesotho) were renowned for being tender and kind and both these women were exceptional examples. I was well looked after, even cosseted, by Gracie primarily, as Rachel left after some time. A kinder, firmer, but gentler person you could never meet. On reflection, she was probably the greatest influence on my life because in my infancy I spent more time with her than any of my family. Grace Shaorane was to stay as caretaker, maid, and friend to our family and in her later days, to my mother for the next 50 years.

When my parents went off to work in the mornings, to keep me safe I was put in a wire pen with some sand and a hose where I spent many happy hours playing. We had two Rhodesian Ridgeback dogs and when Lassie gave birth to a litter of puppies, they shared my pen, all of us perfectly content.

I am not exactly sure of the circumstances, but someone accidentally poisoned me by leaving an open tin of DDT in or near my pen, some of which I must have consumed, white powder being a great attraction for small hands. I nearly died, so the story goes, but saved myself by vomiting not only the entire contents of my stomach but the majority of its lining as well. This was my first brush with death, but it would not be my last.

The United Party had been in power in South Africa since 1924, led by JBM Hertzog who at the beginning of the Second World War was strongly in favour of South Africa remaining a neutral territory, given his firm refusal to enter a European war against Nazi Germany. He was quickly replaced on September 6 1939 by Field Marshal Jan Smuts who immediately committed South Africa to the conflict by declaring war on Germany. By doing so he made himself and his supporters an enemy of the Nationalist Party which was strongly pro-Germany. The United Party under the leadership of General Smuts remained in power until they were deposed by the Nationalist Party led by DF Malan on June 6 1948.

The Nationalist party was determined to introduce apartheid, the total segregation of the population by race. My parents were United Party supporters and admired General Smuts with his policy of unifying all South Africa, both black and white. Consequently, once my father had graduated from Potchefstroom and in theory could now run a farm, he decided to look north of the South African border to the Rhodesias, Northern and Southern, both British territories, although Southern Rhodesia had been self-governing since 1923. It also meant that ex-servicemen could qualify for a settler farm in Southern Rhodesia. However, my parents decided to buy their own property from the Native Commission in the south western corner of Northern Rhodesia, where there were no settler farm deals as the country was still a British protectorate. The purchase of 3,000 acres of virgin African land was secured at the price of ten shillings an acre for a total of 1,500 pounds. In late 1950, they sold the small holding in Johannesburg, and loaded all our possessions into the back of a Ford V8 truck with a canopy over the open tray for us to sleep in along the way. With Gracie and me in the back we set off to start a new life on our recently purchased farm. We arrived on Honeydew Farm, the name we had given our farm after the suburb we had left in Johannesburg, in December 1950. Honeydew was about 20 miles from a small town called Kalomo, which in the early 1900s had been the capital of Northern Rhodesia. In turn the town was about 80 miles to the north of Livingstone and the Victoria Falls on the great Zambezi river.

The farmland was termed savannah, undulating terrain with the ridge lines covered in bush and trees, mainly *mopani* and the troughs covered in grass which would grow long and high enough after the rains to be used as thatch for the roofs of our rudimentary huts. No one lived on the property which meant we did not displace any native or indigenous person with our purchase and arrival. Today, a general but inaccurate belief prevails that when white settlers arrived to farm various parts of central Africa they displaced the native population to do so. Not true. A few small settlements lay close to the railway line which was part of Cecil Rhodes' dream to link Cape Town and Cairo by rail.

When we arrived, the railway line had reached the minerally rich Copperbelt in the north of the country, passing some 14 to 15 miles away from us. My father visited some of the local settlements and the nearest town, Kalomo, to recruit a labour force to get us started. Additionally, soon after arriving we had a drilling company come in to drill a borehole to provide our lifeblood, water. Quick to follow came the task of building sufficient shelter for the whole family and staff.

In those days, settlers and locals alike built houses by sinking poles, cut from the surrounding trees, next to each other in the earth to make a basic, gap-filled wall which we would then fill with a mud mortar mixed from the soil of the many termite mounds, known locally as ant heaps. The gaps filled, you could plaster or render the walls to make a neat clean surface area which, once dried, could be whitewashed or painted. Builders then placed poles conically on top of the walls to provide the framework for a roof which was then covered with thatched grass obtained from the *vleis* or *dambos* as we called them. They were flat, low-lying grassland areas which during the rains would fill up and become wide, shallow streams. In earlier days the shelters would have been known as daub and wattle huts but we preferred the colloquial term of pole and dagga.

Food was basic but abundant with small antelope and guineafowl roaming the surrounding land. My parents used the rifle and shotgun to provide adequate meat for ourselves and the labour force since we had yet to acquire our first herd of cattle. Because the bush and undergrowth were thick, birds in flight were difficult to locate. The preferred method was to load the shotgun with birdshot cartridges and stalk what is properly known as a confusion of guineafowl feeding together, hoping to bag more than one bird at a time. My mother, slight, but strong and determined, made herself the local champion when, with as much luck as marksmanship, she accounted for three birds with a single shot. Her feat made her a figure of awe to the farm labour force.

Snakes and eagles were also regular targets since both displayed an enthusiastic appetite for the smaller dogs and cats that we seemed to have collected. The threat to people was no less real. Several dangerous species of snake inhabited the bush around us. The black mamba, for example, is one of the deadliest and most aggressive snakes in Africa. It takes its name, not from its external colouring, but from the dark grey to black lining of the inside of its mouth. Untreated, its neurotoxic venom takes effect within minutes and death can follow within hours.

On one occasion, two black mamba snakes came swaying through the grass outside the house where I was playing. Tony, fully aware of the risk, rushed off to fetch the shotgun and despatched both before they could pose a further threat to us all. The memory of the adrenalin-based fear as he ran away from me to locate the weapon, leaving me between the snakes and himself, is still with me today.

Some distance away from the main buildings sat a small hut with a toilet seat positioned on top of a large wooden box, which in turn perched over a fathomless hole dug for our toilet. This was regularly doused with lime to contain the smell especially in the summer months. Visits to the *piccaninny kiah* (small house)—still referred to as the PK to this day by people who grew up as we did—became a parade during the night. You needed an escort to hold a lamp as well as look out for snakes and other hazards. For liquid relief, the male population for the most part would irrigate a tree or the grass and to this day many maintain the tradition.

We used paraffin lamps for lighting, igniting a fuel-soaked wick, or pressurising the paraffin into a fine vapour fed into a thin fabric mantle. The Tilley lamp would hiss quietly in the background, providing a gentle but adequate glow. We had no electricity in the house until I was well into my teens.

My parents built themselves a square hut which was attached at one end to the dining room, while Gracie and I shared a small round hut called a rondavel. Late October and early November in central Africa herald the onset of the rainy season which lasts until late February or early March. We had arrived at the beginning of the rains which can be torrential at times, with towering black thunderclouds and tremendous streaks of lightning. Unsurprisingly the roofs of our huts leaked copiously and constantly. We positioned buckets strategically around the floors to capture the rainwater which was much softer and clearer than the more mineralised water from our borehole, and prized for personal bathing. Such was our life for the next few years while the task of making the farm productive continued.

We grew Virginia tobacco which went mainly to the manufacture of cigarettes rather than cigars. To plant the crop, trees had to be cleared, and the land ploughed and furrowed ready for the young seedlings. Huge barns had to be built to heat-cure the tobacco leaf once it was ripe and picked. We planted maize for our own and local consumption and bought as many cattle as we could afford to provide meat and milk for us and the labour force. By the mid to late 1950s the farm consisted of some 80 acres of tobacco, 200 acres of maize, and grazed about 500 head of cattle. To help run the farm we recruited over the years about 60 labourers from all over the country, all of whom built their own huts in the area set aside for their use. They brought their wives, some of whom also performed light labour duties. Many of them brought or later produced numbers of children, so a small community thrived on the farm.

My mother ran a morning clinic three times a week to attend to the many and varied ailments, dispensing codeine, aspirin, cough mixture, malaria tablets, and occasionally a penicillin injection. She also conducted a clinic in Kalomo for the community which she attended three or four times a week. Like the rest of Africa, Northern Rhodesia had many different tribes, speaking more than 20 different languages, none of which my mother could understand or converse in. Despite the obstacle, she became a superb diagnostician without being able to ask the normal questions necessary for a doctor to be able to establish an accurate diagnosis. For more serious cases she would have to transport or send the patients to the nearest hospitals which were 50 and 80 miles away respectively. We all managed a basic lingua franca with the labourers since many of them had worked on the gold mines in South Africa. There, a hybrid language had emerged, a mixture of Afrikaans, Zulu, Xhosa, Swahili, Nyanja, Tonga, and English colloquially termed *fanagalo* or *chilapalapa*. Today the language has virtually disappeared; it is now deemed politically incorrect as a bastardised colonial relic.

Dawn and dusk were consistently at six in the morning and six in the evening. My father would get up every morning at 5:30 to conduct roll call and allocate the tasks for the day. I used to accompany him every morning as the sun came up, chatting away to all those present in Tonga, the local language in which I was now fluent, having been conversing and playing all day with my two young friends, Amon and Aggai who would take me into the *dambos* where we would make clay animals out of the mud or construct skeletal vehicles out of wire with polish tin lids for wheels.

However, the environment was basically hostile for recently arrived Europeans, especially for those with small children, and we all caught malaria. Mosquitoes were rife at this time of year because of the amount of standing water in which they could breed prolifically. My immune system must have been low; I caught every bug going around and went down with malaria badly on a couple of occasions, once requiring Dad to drive to Livingstone 80 miles away in the early hours of the morning to get the necessary drugs to keep me alive.

CHAPTER THREE

Heat and dust, ice and snow

My parents split up 20 years after they married. To this day, I am not sure whether my presence and continued ill health initiated or contributed to their subsequent rift, or whether they were genuinely worried I might die. In any case, they embarked upon a plan of which I was completely oblivious.

One day my mother, with help from an unusually subdued Gracie, packed a suitcase with all my clothes and more, as well as packing a case for herself, telling me we were off on an adventure, ostensibly to visit my grandparents. My father drove us to the local railway siding where we caught the train and two days later arrived in Johannesburg, staying with a farm neighbour's parents. Our neighbour's father—a lovely gentleman—I learned had played cricket for South Africa, making him a giant in my boyish eyes. I can still recall the noise of the traffic sounding just like the roar of the Victoria Falls which we used to visit regularly on our visits to Livingstone.

My parents had told me we were coming to Johannesburg to stay with my grandparents, but somehow it failed to register on the scale of magnitude it should have in my young mind. No doubt these lovely people with whom we were staying were grandparents, but were they actually mine? After a couple of days, surely it was time to go home to the farm and play with my mates, Amon and Aggai. It was not to be. The following day my mother took me to the airport and on the apron in front of what seemed to my eyes an enormous aeroplane, handed me over to a lady dressed in a blue uniform and told me to be a good boy with my grandparents. As to who the real grandparents were, I had no idea. The bewilderment I felt at my situation drove me to despairing tears as my mother turned away and walked out of my life.

The plane was part of the Dutch airline KLM's fleet. I could not know then the role it would play in my later life. All I knew was a sense of abandonment as the air hostesses took over this distraught, un-accompanied minor for the next two days. We stopped overnight in Malta, staying in a hotel on the island and I calmed down considerably when I was allowed to order tomato soup for dinner.

We arrived in Amsterdam on a November afternoon with snow covering the airport apron, a most unusual visual and physical sensation for this young child so accustomed to chalk-dry or steamy-wet Africa. I was introduced to an elderly gentleman who informed me he was my grandfather and that we had to board another aircraft to fly to Manchester, an airport close to his hometown of Preston in Lancashire, England. We arrived at my grandparents' house in the evening, and I was further introduced to a kindly old lady who informed me that she was my grandmother and that I would be living with them for some time. They told me I could call them Granny and Grandpa, to which I had no objection.

I had stopped feeling sorry for myself by now and regaled them with stories of how we would regularly kill and eat lions at home. It was snug and warm in their house and what was more, I could see everything at night because they controlled a magical phenomenon called electricity which, with the flick of a switch, lit up the whole room. Amazing! The best part of my new life was the comforting presence of a large dog called Rock with whom I immediately formed an alliance. I could relate to dogs. Humans were the strange ones.

Grandpa Will went off to work the next day and Granny Elsie set up a little pretend office in the lounge for me so I too could go to work. Each day I was allowed to change the ivory cards in a holder showing the month, day, and date. Life and my self-esteem were certainly improving; I too had a job to go to every morning. Soon after my arrival, Granny took me for a ride on a strange red machine called a double decker bus, run by the Ribble Bus Company. I sat upstairs in the front of the bus as we crossed the bridge over the River Ribble on our way into Preston. She took me to an outfitter who ceremonially swathed me in grey—grey shorts, grey shirt, and grey stockings. A red blazer was added, and a grey hat with a red hat band. I was yet to understand that my mornings of mock employment would give way to attendance at an institution called school.

At Woodlands School I underwent yet another new experience—meeting large numbers of white children when my friends and playmates at home were black. But life soon settled into a regular routine. On Saturdays, Grandpa used to take me to his club where he loved playing snooker or billiards with his friends.

Occasionally, we would drive to Blackpool for lunch which suited me perfectly provided our table came equipped with a bottle of tomato sauce. Tomato soup too was always on the menu. We would occasionally visit the Trough of Bowland which sticks in my memory to this day as verdant and beautiful. I also grew accustomed to the snow that fell each winter I was there. I soon forgot about those people called parents.

My maternal aunts, Wendy Rodwell and Margaret Poulter, came for a visit. Wendy was getting married to Bob Phillips, an actuary whom she had met while studying at Cambridge, and Margaret was her bridesmaid. I spoiled the filming of the event by running in front of the camera and pulling ridiculous faces. Margaret stayed on for a time after the wedding. Her husband, Ralph Poulter, was a farmer in Rhodesia, and being so far away I think she was homesick. Aside from her wedding duties, another of her tasks was to escort me back to Africa.

I have no recollection of saying goodbye to my grandparents or to Rock. I do recall sitting next to Aunt Margaret on the aircraft, and her telling me that the next stop was Lusaka where she would leave me, to be met by parents while she continued on to Salisbury to re-join her husband, Ralph, and return to their farm close by. She and the aircraft duly departed while I sat on the steps of the airport terminal building with no evidence of parents in attendance. I squatted contentedly watching the world go by. A couple, clearly flustered, rushed straight past me up the airport steps. They seemed somehow both familiar yet unconnected. After some time, these relative strangers dashed back and flung their arms around me. They informed me they were my parents.

'Who and what were parents?' I wondered in my seven-year-old way; it was nearly two years since I had last seen them. I haughtily inform-ed them I could eat with a knife and fork.

'I should expect so,' retorted my alleged mother.

That wasn't very friendly, I thought.

CHAPTER FOUR

A stranger at home and at school

I'd returned to Africa. But the virtual infant of five years who had left in such innocence two years before was the not the same seven year old boy making his way back to paradise.

Our journey in the Ford V8 vanette along a well graded dirt road took six hours. (The drive back to the farm today on a sealed but broken and pot-holed surface would take the same time.) As darkness fell, we sustained a puncture, with my father having to change the wheel by the side of the road. I refused to get out of the vehicle. The little hero who amused his grandparents with tales of killing and eating lions had lost his bravado. There really *were* lions in Africa and they definitely ate people.

Home now was a brick building and I had my own room. Although I could remember her more clearly than my own parents, there was no Gracie with whom to share. She had her own house. Many more unfamiliar dogs and cats shared our residence. My father woke me the next morning to attend the roll call, a ritual that once seemed as natural as breathing. Now it was cold, and dark, and alien, and suddenly I was surrounded by grinning faces jabbering at me in an impenetrable tongue. I clung to my father's legs, and gaped at these raucous figures in terror. They shook their heads in bewilderment. What had happened to this child, their friend who used to play, laugh, and sing with them as one of their own? Who was this stranger, this...ghost?

My life had changed for ever. Fear and under-confidence lurked like a shadow in my subconscious for years. Sadly, I never spoke fluent Tonga again. Although I was not an unhappy child, I was certainly introverted, generating my own amusement and activity from within. As young boys growing up on a farm, we were all fascinated with the many mechanical implements needed and I was no exception, learning to drive the tractors as soon as my feet could reach the clutch and brake pedals. As I grew bigger and older, during my school holidays I would work a full day on the tractor, hauling the trailer, pulling tree stumps out of newly cleared land, and ploughing or disking. The task that gave me the greatest satisfaction was ploughing. I derived enormous pleasure from turning the earth in dead-straight, even furrows with symmetrical, wave-like curls of the soil. Later, I'd use the disk plough to level and smooth the entire field, leaving it resembling a flat tabletop in the middle of the African bush.

Agricultural shows were held throughout the country. Lusaka, the capital city, hosted the biggest and most important event where farmers could display anything from livestock to crops. Accompanying my father one year, I found myself bored looking at hundreds of cattle and wandered off to the mechanical section where producers and distributors exhibited their latest hardware. To encourage the young, the Fordson tractor brand staged a tractor driving competition. I entered and to my astonishment won, while driving a type of machine completely new to me; my first competitive success. When my father later asked what I'd been up to, he was surprised and delighted with my accomplishment.

School, of course, had to continue. The local school in Kalomo was nearly 20 miles away, making it impossible for my parents to drive me every day, so my mother, on her way to her work at the clinic on

Monday would drop me off and collect me on the following Friday afternoon. Kalomo primary was a day school, so I boarded with various families in the town. One was a Jewish couple who ran the local hardware store, Scherr and Behrens. Scylla and Heinz Behrens were a delightful, gentle, and kind pair.

Preparing to extract me from the bath, Scylla rolled up her long sleeves and I noticed a lengthy set of numbers along her arm. When I asked her what they meant, she quickly rolled her sleeves back down and told me they were of no importance. Years later I learned she had survived incarceration in one of the notorious German concentration camps, either Auschwitz or Birkenau, and still bore the tattooed reminder of her prison identity number the German SS gave her, and millions like her.

After the war, many European refugees sought a new life in a peaceful but rewarding environment by emigrating to the Rhodesias. The local schools in central Africa had pupils of many different backgrounds. Among them were Armenians such as the Amieras—Tucky and his attractive sister Marooshka. Exotic surnames such as De Goveia, Borejzso, Posthma, and others intrigued us.

Our small Kalomo farming community also contained a decent number of experienced, battle-hardened war heroes. They included characters such as Peter Corbishley, a group captain in the RAF who flew photo reconnaissance Mosquito aircraft, often unarmed to lighten their load, allowing them to fly higher and further over Germany. George Buchanan won a Distinguished Flying Cross (DFC) and had gained a reputation as a fighter ace in Malta, shooting down several German aircraft. Syd Middleton was a major in a tank regiment with the Eighth Army. Neville Bowker, the third highest scoring fighter ace from Rhodesia, was eventually shot down and captured by the Germans, spending the rest of the war in Stalag Luft III, a notorious prisoner of war camp for Allied airmen. The prison was pivotal to two fictionalised post-war films, *The Wooden Horse*, and *The Great Escape*, loosely telling the stories of escapes from the camp. Then there were the three Daphne brothers, David, ex-army, Tony, ex-navy and Peter, ex-RAF. Their mother insisted they went into separate services in the belief that the strategy would improve their chances of survival. I'm sure I have missed others who distinguished themselves during the war but in a small community it was remarkable how many were heroes.

After a few months my mother secured a place for me at Codrington, a junior boarding school in Mazabuka some four hours to the north. Named after a previous governor of Northern Rhodesia, the majority of the boarders hailed from outlying farm communities, so we mostly shared the same outlook on life and behaviour. We were all boys, whereas the day scholars who joined us in the classroom during the week were mainly girls.

We all ate in the communal dining hall and slept in dormitories under the fierce monitoring of two formidable women, Matrons Saunders and Anderson. Every morning at breakfast we had to take a little pill waiting for us on our side plate. Paludrine, a malaria prophylactic, was a bitter little pill which needed copious amounts of liquid to wash it down and prevent it sticking to your tongue or your mouth, causing much involuntary shuddering.

I spent five fairly uneventful years at Codrington. Our holidays lasted for three weeks twice a year and six weeks over Christmas when we could return to our families, otherwise we never saw them. Northern Rhodesia was an enthusiastic member of the British Commonwealth and we would celebrate Commonwealth Day, Armistice Day, and others by dressing in our smartest uniforms and marching under supervision into town. We would stand at attention while the Union Jack was raised, and the band played the British national anthem.

The weekends were free of academic work. On Saturday we were allowed into town to spend our pocket money. A shilling in those days could buy any number of sweets and sherbets. Saturday was also team sport day; we would bus to towns as far away as Lusaka to play cricket or football.

Sunday school was compulsory after breakfast, when we would receive visits by the Salvation Army, mostly Americans who would regale us with stories of Jesus turning water into wine, restoring mobility to the lame, and even returning from death to life himself. It was impressive. In the afternoon the matrons or deputy head would organise sessions of 'gloves'. If any of us had a gripe with another pupil we could settle our differences by each donning a pair of boxing gloves and bash away at each other until either you or your opponent yielded. One Sunday, for no particular reason, I decided that Chalen Posthma, a perfectly genial young fellow, needed me to teach him a lesson and I challenged him to don gloves. He did so, though with an expression that combined amusement and bemusement. He was twice my size, and of Hawaiian extraction. After a few exchanges between David and Goliath, the matron rushed in to rescue this splayed, breathless child from any further punishment. What lesson I delivered or received, I wasn't quite sure, but once recovered, I determined to only pick a fight or a battle that I was confident I would win. Chalen and I, however, remained good friends for the rest of his time at the school.

Coming from an agricultural background, the school expected us to belong to the Young Farmers' Club where, below the football pitch, we had a series of allotments where we could grow vegetables. I cannot remember having any great success, although I spent considerable time there enjoying peace away from the usual crowd. Throughout my time at Codrington we all adopted various crazes that thrived for a while before we moved on to the next. From this distance, marbles and jacks were the most popular.

One incident affected me deeply for a considerable part of my early life. At night, once in bed in the dormitory, lights out and absolute silence were strictly enforced. However, put a group of young children together and the temptation to socialise is all but irresistible. An irate matron or master would invariably interrupt the high spirits and hilarious stories, switching the lights on and instantly identifying the culprits for subsequent punishment.

In later days such misdemeanours resulted in a caning. The use of the cane was part of the punishment process throughout the second half of my school career. On one occasion when I was just 11 years old, after lights out a boy shone a torch against the white wall while other boys intertwined their fingers in the beam making shadows of rabbits, dogs, and other animals. I had an idea to liven things up by dropping my pyjama pants and dangling my little willie in the beam. The magnification of my shadowed member threw everyone into raucous hysterics. It also brought the world as I knew it—or at least my sense of justice—to a crashing close.

The dorm lights snapped on and a furious headmaster, Mr O'Connell, a devout Catholic, stood there glaring. He announced to this by now terrified child, 'I know exactly what you were doing, and I will deal with you tomorrow.' A sleepless night followed. I decided that a wise plan would involve running away, stealing a ride on a train to the Copperbelt, and disappearing for good.

The next day the news was out, and all the girls in my classroom were tittering and casting me odd glances. Eventually, during class, the boy who owned the torch was called and told to report to the headmaster's study. He returned stifling tears of pain. Now it was my turn. The head asked me what my parents would think if they knew what I had been up to. I found it difficult to think, let alone answer. What seemed like the mildest morsel of mischief had suddenly transformed into a dark and terrible felony. After a pause of a second or two that felt like a year, he declared he was not going to expel me but the punishment needed to fit the crime. I was made to bend over and prepare to receive six of the best. Half a dozen cuts with a bamboo cane across my now tense buttocks in the touch-your-toes position may sound relatively mild to an adult accustomed to bruising reality. But to an innocent nurtured in the warmth of a caring family, this assault came as a violent shock. The first stroke was excruciatingly painful, all but taking my breath away. But the real challenge was to avoid crying, because at least then, once the punishment was complete, I could turn to my persecutor and thank him, providing myself with the semblance of a moral victory. On my return to the classroom both Keith (the boy with the torch) and I were accorded a semi-heroic status for a time.

My issue then, and one which still troubles me, is what this unfortunate man really believed we were up to with our childish game. I raged about the injustice of an accusation I didn't fully understand, and the severity of the punishment attached to it. How, I wondered, could a system meant to impart values such as love and care invest such brutal power in those charged with teaching them?

Nursing my wounded dignity and pride, I looked forward to holidays on the farm for solace. When I was not driving the tractors, I amused myself by playing pretend cricket matches between England and South Africa, bouncing the cricket ball off a wall and elegantly fending it away from the wickets (three sticks driven into the dirt). Self-taught athletics also took up some of my time and imagination as I fantasised about my passage to the Olympics. I had a heavy (for me) and smooth round rock the size of a large grapefruit which became a shot putt, while my fishing spear doubled as my javelin.

Our school year concluded with the long Christmas holidays, but in the mid-year break of my fifth year at Codrington my parents told me I was not returning to the school. The news was a blow since I was beginning to make real progress. I was in the first team for soccer and cricket and doing well at athletics. Equally painful was missing the chance to say goodbye to most of my friends. I learned that my parents had enrolled me in the private boarding school system in Southern Rhodesia, whose terms followed the September to July school year of the United Kingdom, rather than January to December. They drove me more than 400 miles to a school called Peterhouse just outside a small town named Marandellas (today Marondera) where I was to spend the next seven years of my life.

Pictured clockwise: 1) Sandspruit Farm, Honeydew, outside Johannesburg, 1947, where my father's post-war farming career began. **2)** My father, Bruce Rodwell, and me, South Africa, 1949, the year prior to starting life on the farm in then Northern Rhodesia (Zambia). **3)** Me with Gracie Shaorane and Rachel, 1949. Gentle Gracie would go on to accompany my mother as a domestic worker, caretaker, and friend for another 50 years. **4)** Me with my mother, Dr Pat Goddard, 1950. In those days, the law demanded a female doctor retain the surname under which she had qualified.

Pictured clockwise: 1) My mother, Pat with her first son and my half-brother, Tony Aldridge. Her first husband, Dr Barney Aldridge, was captured by the Japanese at the fall of Singapore, and executed soon after for want of space in a prisoner of war camp. 2) Setting up camp. The earliest days on Honeydew, 1951. 3) My father and a drilling contractor with the first bore water on Honeydew, 1951 Although our ramshackle huts leaked constantly, we collected the rainwater for personal bathing, preferring it to the mineralised bore variety. 4) *Top and centre:* Thatched pole and *dagga* (mud) huts provide rudimentary shelter in the early days on the farm; *bottom:* Farm pals, Amon and Aggai. Until my parents sent me to live in England aged five, I had only black friends and playmates.

Pictured clockwise: 1) *top:* My companion, Aggai, and me on Honeydew Farm, near Kalomo, Northern Rhodesia (Zambia) circa 1953. *bottom:* Collecting eggs on the farm, 1953. **2)** Eleanor and her seven piglets, circa 1953. For the first months on the farm, we lived off the land, shooting guinea fowl and buck for the family and staff. Livestock came later. **3)** My mother and brother, Tony, with our Rhodesian Ridgebacks on the farm, 1953. **4)** Tony (right, with weapon) and an unidentified farm hand display Tony's victims: two deadly black mambas seen heading my way as a child around 1953.

Pictured clockwise: 1) Grandpa Will and Granny Elsie Rodwell at their home in Preston, England, with Rock the hound in 1954. I could relate to dogs. Humans were the odd ones. **2)** The hunter home from the hill. The rifle is bigger than me, but I'm just a little proud to pretend to have despatched a black mamba of my own, following the example of my older brother, Tony. **3)** Our new, permanent home emerges from a rough clearing circa 1956. **4)** The tall tobacco curing barns and the grading shed, 1957.

Pictured clockwise: 1) A woman's work is never done. My mother pitches in to help our cook, Amon, and farm assistant, Alec, dip the ever-growing circus of farm dogs in an anti-tick wash. Behind are the gravity-fed bore water tank, and to the left the household boiler: two 44-gallon drums over a perpetual fire. 2) Local farming families dress up for the Christmas tree celebration at the Kalomo country club, late 1950s. 3) Me at Codrington School, Northern Rhodesia, shortly before being sent to Peterhouse in Southern Rhodesia 1959.

Pictured clockwise: 1) A fine specimen of a Brahman bull enjoying the lush grazing we created from the bush in the 1950s and 60s. 2) My father on the veranda of the now well-established farm and garden in the 1960s. 3) Rain-laden clouds and rising river levels mark the end of the dust-choked dry and the onset of the rainy season. The road to the farm is impassable after a heavy storm in 1959. 4) Another view of the swollen Maziba River over the farm bridge.

Pictured clockwise: 1) Leaves of green and gold. Central Africa provided some of the best conditions on the planet for growing tobacco and maize. My father grew his first crop in the early1960s. **2)** Both Northern and Southern Rhodesia held enviable international reputations for the quality of their livestock, especially beef cattle. At its height, Honeydew carried about 500 head of cattle. **3)** Cattle are herded through a spray to protect them from life-threatening ticks, tsetse flies, and other pests. **4)** Hard work and a determined vision created a peaceful and comfortable oasis for a boy in the African bush.

Pictured clockwise: 1) African farming is a constant battle with nature. A cow is rounded up for inoculation against the myriad diseases prevalent among the cattle in central Africa. 2) Family life. Aged 12 on school holidays on the farm with its now luxuriant garden. 3) Driven. My interest in machinery began early. I drove the tractor on the farm as soon as my feet could reach the pedals.

CHAPTER FIVE

Big school, big lessons, big history

Peterhouse was one of Southern Rhodesia's top schools, a private college comparable to those of the so-called public schools in the UK. It received no government subsidy, with families paying princely sums of money to keep the school solvent. Other great schools in Salisbury (Harare), Umtali (Mutare), Bulawayo, and various other towns were deemed Government institutions because the state largely funded them with minimal contribution from the parents. Our headmaster (or rector) was a forward-thinking educationalist who had taught in India and subsequently been the rector at Michaelhouse, acknowledged as one of the top private schools in South Africa, before coming to Rhodesia and founding Peterhouse.

Frederick Snell was a rector of whom, initially, we were terrified. Small in stature but with a penetrating stare and an astute understanding of the young, he was to have a great influence on me. I regard him as one the wisest men I have had the pleasure to meet. After I left school and he had retired locally, we were privileged as a family to have him and his wife, Margaret, to Sunday lunch on several occasions.

Peterhouse was an all-boys school containing five boarding houses with between 50 and 60 boys accommodated in each. A housemaster and his deputy supervised and monitored activities of the house and its occupants during the day but handed over control to the head of house and his student prefects from the evening until the next morning after breakfast.

Peterhouse was a progressive Anglican Christian school. Towards the end of my time there it arranged the inclusion of black pupils, the first school in the country to do so.

The school motto *Conditur in Petra*, (founded on a rock) engendered the ethos of a sound Christian foundation, combined with developing an independent mind and critical thinking. Choosing to be a 'reggie' (a conformist) was, in today's parlance, uncool. We were a close-knit, tightly-bonded group of young men. These strong ties have weathered the ages with many of my school mates still among my closest friends today. Many were considered mavericks, in keeping with the mood of the country which was about to rebel against the motherland, Great Britain, by announcing a unilateral declaration of independence (UDI). More of that later, but certainly I learned quickly there are consequences, good and bad, to every course of action or behaviour.

I did not particularly distinguish myself academically but achieved the minimum requirements to apply to join the Royal Air Force in the UK. On the other hand, I loved sport and was awarded school colours for rugby, athletics, squash, and basketball.

CHAPTER SIX

Behind the looking glass —Southern Rhodesia to Zimbabwe

Rhodesia, was named after Cecil John Rhodes, the British empire-builder who was one of the most important figures in British expansion into southern Africa. He obtained extensive mineral rights in 1888 from the most powerful local traditional leaders through treaties signed by King Lobengula, leader of the Ndebele tribe. The Ndebele were the predominant tribe of the territory to the south of the Zambezi River, and were originally part of the powerful Zulu nation of South Africa. The British government agreed that Rhodes' business entity, the British South Africa Company (BSAC), would receive exclusive mineral rights over the lands stretching from the Limpopo River to Lake Tanganyika, with Queen Victoria signing the charter in 1889. Southern Rhodesia became a self-governing British Crown Colony in 1923, derived from British South Africa Company territories lying south of the Zambezi River. The British South Africa Company governed various parts of the country to the north of the Zambezi in the late 1890s, after which the whole territory became known as Northern Rhodesia, and the territory to its east, Nyasaland.

Britain had granted self-governing status to Rhodesia as far back as 1923, recognising the local administrative system was well advanced. In 1953, with calls for independence mounting in many of its African colonies, the United Kingdom created the Federation of Rhodesia and Nyasaland (or the Central African Federation, CAF) which consisted of Southern Rhodesia, Northern Rhodesia, and Nyasaland (now Zimbabwe, Zambia, and Malawi, respectively). In persuading Rhodesia to join the federation, the carrot was a promise of independence should the venture fail or the CAF dissolve. It goes some way towards explaining the subsequent anger of the Rhodesians (now Southern Rhodesia within the CAF). Those interested in the history of the era should examine Ian Smith's book *The Great Betrayal.*

The idea was to try to steer a middle road between the differing aspirations of black nationalists, the colonial administration, and the white settler population. The federation sought to emulate the experience of Australia, Canada, and South Africa, where groups of colonies had joined together to form viable independent nations. Originally designed to be 'an indissoluble federation', the CAF quickly began to unravel due to the low proportion of British and other white citizens in relation to the larger black populations, and the stresses arising through unequal land, wealth, and power distribution. Additionally, by incorporating the tribes within the federation as potential citizens, the federation created the paradox of having a white elite owning most of the land and capital, while using cheap black labour.

During World War Two, Southern Rhodesian military units fought on the side of Britain. Southern Rhodesian forces were involved on many fronts including the east and north African campaigns, Italy, Madagascar and Burma. Southern Rhodesian forces had the highest loss ratio of any constituent element, colony, dependency, or dominion of the British Empire forces during World War Two. Additionally, Rhodesian pilots earned the highest number of decorations and ace titles of any group within the empire. This national contribution resulted in the royal family paying an unusual state visit to the colony at the end of the war to thank the Rhodesian people.

Southern Rhodesia developed an economy narrowly based on production of a few primary products, notably chrome and tobacco. It was therefore vulnerable to classical economic cycles. The deep depression of the 1930s gave way to a post-war boom. This surge prompted the immigration of about 200,000 white settlers between 1945 and 1970, expanding the white population to 307,000. Many of these immigrants were of British working-class origin. More settlers from the Belgian Congo, Kenya, Tanzania, and later Angola and Mozambique, as well as an increased birth rate, raised the Rhodesian white population to around 600,000 by 1976. The black population was about six million.

The Federation of Rhodesia and Nyasaland was dissolved on January 1 1964. However, it was expected that only Nyasaland would be let go, while the remainder of Rhodesia, both north and south, would remain united. Although Northern Rhodesia had a white population of more than 100,000, as well as additional British military and civilian residents and their dependents, most of these were relatively new to the region, were primarily involved in the extraction industry, had little landed interests, and were more tolerant of black nationalism than the Southern Rhodesians. Accordingly, Britain granted independence to Northern Rhodesia on October 24 1964. However, when the new nationalists changed its name to Zambia and began an initially tentative and later more rapid Africanisation campaign, Southern Rhodesia chose to remain a British colony, resisting attempts to introduce majority rule. The colony attempted to change its name to Rhodesia, a proposal the United Kingdom rejected. The majority of the federation's military and financial assets went to Southern Rhodesia, since the British Government did not wish to see them fall into the hands of the nationalist leaders, and because Southern Rhodesia had borne the major expenses of running the federation. However, due to its vast copper deposits, Northern Rhodesia was the wealthiest of the three member states and had contributed more to the overall building of infrastructure than the other two members. Southern Rhodesia, anticipating an inevitable dissolution of the federation, was quick to use federal funds to build its infrastructure ahead of the others. A key component of this wave of development was the building of the vast Kariba dam and its hydroelectric facility, located on the Southern Rhodesian side of the Zambezi Gorge.

With the protectorate of Northern Rhodesia dissolved, in 1964 Southern Rhodesia reverted to the name Rhodesia. In 1965, Rhodesia unilaterally declared itself independent of Britain, under a white-dominated government led by Ian Smith. After a long civil war between the white (until 1979) government and two African majority, Soviet-bloc and Chinese-aligned liberation movements (Zimbabwe People's Revolutionary Army and Zimbabwe African National Liberation Army), Britain resumed control for a brief period before granting independence to the country in 1980, whereupon it became Zimbabwe.

When we arrived on Honeydew Farm in 1950, Britain effectively governed us through the Colonial Service until 1953. With the formation of the Central African Federation, the Federal Government in Salisbury, the capital, took progressively more control.

Collectively we were a proud group of citizens, both black and white, who for the most part had been brought together as a consequence of the Second World War. All were trying to make a success of our new lives, and to all intents and purposes, it worked at the time. Northern Rhodesians were, however, wary of their southern neighbours. They believed they possessed more abundant and lucrative resources which, to their eyes, appeared to benefit the south disproportionately. The African name given to Salisbury—*bamba zonke* (take all)—was thought appropriate by many in the north. However, the British Commonwealth and many other nations viewed Southern Rhodesia as an efficient and well run country whose infrastructure and administration services were second to none at the time.

It was for a while a mostly harmonious and happy existence for all. Housing, medical care, and schooling were free for the black population. Their children received free education through a combination of farm and government funded schools. In 1980, when Rhodesia became Zimbabwe, every young person in the country had received an education to at least standard six level and many beyond. This was a record in any colony or protectorate, with a literacy rate among the highest in the Commonwealth.

In the early 1960s the atmosphere in Northern Rhodesia began to change as the growing dissatisfaction of black nationalists, who were pushing hard for majority rule, became increasingly aggressive. Life on the farm grew more and more difficult. The labour force was under pressure to take a stance against white rule. Some were exhorted, even threatened, to commit acts of blatant terror against their colleagues who thought and behaved differently.

Under the circumstances, my mother made the decision to move. Despite her contribution to the local community, black activists displayed an increasing hostility to all whites, making it impossible for her to continue her medical duties unhindered. At the same time, our next door farming neighbours, my god parents, Gordon and Norah Brooks, had been driven off their farm. Gordon had secured the post of engineering manager at the Kamativi tin mine in western Rhodesia. He advised my mother the position of chief medical officer was vacant. She applied for the job and was accepted. The time was right to effect an exit from a rapidly disintegrating Zambia.

My father stayed on the farm trying to make it work under increasingly arduous circumstances; the infrastructure of the new Zambia had all but collapsed in the space of three years. He commuted between the farm and Kamativi whenever he could, but my mother never visited the farm again. The memory of what she had built up and lost was too hard for her to bear. I spent less and less of my holiday time on the farm too, since the social and sporting life on the mine provided a stark contrast to the now lonely existence of Zambian rural life. My father found farming tougher and tougher. It became virtually impossible to manage daily operations. Spare parts for machinery were scarce or unobtainable. The railway ceased to function. The telephone system had broken down and the work force laboured under continual harassment or caused problems through their own political motivations. After a few years he managed to sell the farm for a pittance but was able to recover most of the farm equipment and transport it across the border into Rhodesia (which it had now become after the breakup of the CAF). He bought a coffee farm in the eastern highlands of the country outside a small town called Chipinga (now Chipinge).

Commuting between Kamativi and Chipinga became more difficult as well. By this time I had left school and was on my way to the UK to join the Royal Air Force.

CHAPTER SEVEN

Taking flight—the Royal Air Force disaster

While still at Peterhouse, on November 11 1965, staff summoned us to assembly in the main dining hall after lunch. We normally had assembly only at the beginning and end of term, or exceptionally when the rector found it necessary to explain why he was expelling certain pupils. We thought of it as a rare event but one crammed with pageantry. The masters solemnly filed in, draped in full academic regalia from renowned universities including Oxford, Cambridge, London, Rhodes, Cape Town, and others.

Snell brought up the rear, walking slowly but purposefully up to the stage where all the sombre faced masters were already seated. Normally they would converse quietly with each other, and from the assembled boys a hum of chatter would fill the hall. On this occasion utter silence commanded the space. Snell commenced his address, telling us that at 1100 that morning the Prime Minister of Rhodesia had gone ahead with his plans to sever the country's ties with Britain through a unilateral declaration of independence (UDI). He then read the declaration aloud. After a long pause, he announced that 'for everyone in this room your lives will change irrevocably forever'. He would pray for our future and that of the country. He was prophetically correct.

With Zambia already independent, and without the future support of the UK or the federation, the writing of Rhodesia's future appeared large on an increasingly blank wall. My mother's move to Kamativi, and my father's growing struggle to maintain the farm, formed an anxious part of the message.

Britain immediately imposed sanctions against Rhodesia and sent a squadron of fighter aircraft to Lusaka with the intention of bringing its once favourite colonial child to heel.

It was no surprise that many of us at school felt there was no future staying in the country once we had finished our education. At least 90 per cent of the pupils who left Peterhouse over the next two years departed for the UK or South Africa to continue their studies. Very few ever returned to live in Rhodesia. I was no exception and spent the next two years at Peterhouse preparing myself to join the Royal Air Force in the UK. My brother, Tony, was already a great success there, and my close friend, Sam Hunt, a year ahead of me at school, had won a place at the RAF College Cranwell. It seemed a good way to join.

Curiously, although my father owned and flew a small aircraft, his example probably had less influence on my yearning for a career in aviation than might have been expected. I recall it had a tiny, cramped cockpit and he did all the flying. He occasionally piloted me to school from the farm, a hot, bumpy, and uncomfortable five to six hour flight, including a re-fuelling stop in Binga.

To me fighter cockpits were the only way to get into the air. Years later I flew a Piper Vagabond, the type he owned, on a C of A air test. The flight confirmed it was one of my least favourite aircraft to fly.

I finished school in the middle of 1967. By then my mother had moved to Kariba, again as chief medical officer working for the Rhodesian government. My school mates and I were able to spend some pleasant weeks enjoying Lake Kariba—still the world's largest man-made body of water by volume—and all that the local facilities offered. My father brought his speedboat which I would use from time to time to visit the resort hotels. It offered yet another opportunity to put myself in peril.

One sizzling afternoon I decided to visit some friends who ran the Kariba Breezes hotel. Jumping into the boat, I cast off from the mooring and engaged the starter. Regrettably, fuel had leaked into the engine compartment and vapourised in the heat. The spark from the starter motor ignited the fuel vapour and an almighty explosion blew off the engine compartment housing which knocked me into the murky depths of the harbour. All I could do was tread water and watch as my father's boat slowly burned. The manager of the boat yard succeeded in extinguishing the flames, but not before they had reduced the vessel to a charred hull. As he towed the wreck back to his yard, he fished me out of the lake with the dry comment, 'that was pretty stupid'.

'Thanks for the sympathy,' I thought, but held my tongue.

I travelled to Salisbury in September, meeting up with another great school friend, Adrian Hosack, also bound for England. Together we caught the train south to Cape Town. It was a very different train journey from the previous year when we had travelled as the Peterhouse rugby team on a tour of the Cape province schools. Then, girls from our sister school, Arundel, in Salisbury, accompanied us on the train on their own hockey tour to Cape Town. The masters and mistresses of the respective schools had a torrid time trying to keep the two groups apart. Much fun was had and the coincidence of the return journey containing both school teams gave us a pleasant bonus. The trip in each direction took three days and two nights, long enough for current friendships to consolidate and new ones to form.

This time, on arrival in Cape Town, we went straight to the harbour and boarded the *Windsor Castle*, a large passenger liner that would take us to England. The boat ticket cost £90 and the journey took exactly two weeks. We had missed an earlier boat taking all the southern African university students back to the UK, and the only single young lady on the boat spent most of her time in the company of the ship's purser. Adrian and I spent much of our time gambling on the one armed bandit slot machines trying to line up Noughts and Crosses, or Tic Tac Toe in the three small windows and so win the jackpot which would subsidise our lunchtime gin and tonics. The vessel had just two machines, one of which seemed continually occupied by an old dear who regularly won the jackpot, much to our annoyance.

Deck quoits in the afternoon and the occasional swim made for an uneventful crossing. The regular passengers played bridge, took part in the daily mileage tote, and enjoyed a relaxing passage. We young, aspiring pilots were bored stiff.

We shared a four-berth cabin with two South African Lebanese characters known colloquially as the Jo'burg Lebs who were, to that point in my life, the scariest people I had met. They regularly returned to the cabin violently drunk, punched holes in the ceiling for fun, and conducted all their verbal exchanges in a bellicose yell. For reasons known only to themselves, they found me an ideal target on which to vent their boat-bound boredom and displeasure by regularly scaring the life out of me. One evening they amused themselves by dangling me by my ankles over the rails of the ship. While I gagged with horror at the inky black Atlantic below, they wet their pants with mirth at my manifest discomfort.

In the end, I suppose I scored a moral victory. Early in the morning before we docked at Southampton, we were up on deck watching as the Isle of Wight slid past. They asked what they should do with the bundle of hashish they had brought with them to pay their way in England. It would be worth a small fortune on the street. I informed them that the customs officers they were bound to meet employed sniffer dogs who would instantly smell out the contraband and as a result they could expect a couple of years at Her Majesty's pleasure in

Pentonville or Wormwood Scrubs. 'What should we do?' they asked 'Give it to me,' I said, 'and I'll save you from going to prison', promptly throwing their stash overboard. The Lebs were dumbfounded, but I made sure there were plenty of passengers around me to save me from further harm.

Things started off badly on our arrival in gloomy, rain-soaked England. On the train from Southampton to London, I managed to lose Adrian's address book with all his British contacts. Naturally he was furious, but he had a distant aunt whom he thought he could track down. Without adieu, he left me in the middle of London and departed for Maidenhead. We never quite recovered our close friendship after that misfortune. I went up to Norfolk to stay with my brother, Tony, and his family who were based at Coltishall, a famous World War Two fighter station where Tony was instructing on Lightnings. I stayed for a while, getting on their nerves before buying an old Ford Prefect for £50 and setting off to try my fortunes in London. I stayed with various acquaintances and worked at a few casual jobs while waiting for my RAF interview. The longest lasting was as a sausage delivery driver. I was given a smart red van which I used to deliver meat products around southern England.

My selection interview was scheduled for November 1967 and I travelled to Biggin Hill by train on a bleak autumn afternoon. Biggin Hill, another famous World War Two fighter station steeped in history, had a most humbling effect on all of us hopeful air force pilots. I cannot remember a great deal about the five days I spent at the Officers' and Aircrew Selection Centre (OASC). I know the medical team spent a great deal of time probing, measuring, whispering, and X-raying and by the end of the evening those whose names were not called out had passed A1, G1, Z1, the minimum requirement to commence training as a pilot. The train departing for London contained many young men whose dreams of becoming a pilot were already dashed.

The statistics show that of the 70,000 who applied, a mere 0.1 per cent were successful. Those in the intake came to dread the next two evenings. If your name was read out it meant you too must take your disappointed place on the next train to London. The last two days consisted of team exercises, both physical and mental. Come Friday evening, we were all told to wait for a letter from the Ministry of Defence, and sent home.

The interview process was to identify candidates for a position as a flight cadet at the Royal Air Force College Cranwell for two and a half years of training. I thought the RAF would select future leaders from Cranwell, whereas many pilots found their way into the ranks through the direct entry system. In retrospect that is the route I should have taken, but I was not to know at the time, desperate as I was for acceptance into the college.

All successful recruits were offered jobs as General Duties Officers with their specialty in brackets: GD(P) designated a pilot, N as a navigator or E as an engineer. GD(P) was my sole interest and eventually in January I received a letter from the Ministry of Defence accepting me for pilot training as a flight cadet at Cranwell, commencing April 1 1968. Maybe starting on April Fool's day carried a message for me, but that moment represents an exquisitely happy and memorable day in my life.

On the Monday afternoon I caught the train to Grantham in Lincolnshire, dressed in a sports jacket and tie and sporting a fedora hat which was compulsory when we wore civilian clothes. A flight sergeant welcomed us, barking orders and ushering us onto a barber-bound bus for the obligatory short back and sides. The authorities divided the number 98 cadet intake into four squadrons A, B, C, and D whose associated colours were red, yellow, blue and green. The course consisted of five semesters of six months, after which successful participants would graduate with our pilots' wings as pilot officers. We were billeted for the first semester in Nissan huts with four cadets to a hut. We had to keep the hut and everything in it—including ourselves—spotless, which involved regular inspections by the sharp-eyed and frequently sharp-tongued senior entry cadets.

The main college building was, and still is, an impressive structure which we were not allowed to enter for the first year, after which we lived there for the duration of our course.

Our first task was to learn to march, always to the accompaniment of a full brass band. I was in awe of the whole establishment and felt extremely privileged and fortunate to have won selection to this prestigious institution.

As soon as we had learnt the essential mechanics of the de Havilland Chipmunk, we started flying training proper using the grass airstrip to the north of the college building. After about 10 hours of dual instruction most of us were ready to go solo. When your instructor got out of the aircraft, secured his now empty straps to prevent them flapping about, and said, 'off you go', it was the most liberating and exhilarating feeling, one never to be forgotten. I had read countless books about First World War fighter aces, heroes such as 'Mick' Mannock, James McCudden, and Albert Ball, all three of whom had won the Victoria Cross. I had also devoured books about Second World War fighter aces such as 'Sailor' Malan, Robert Stanford Tuck, 'Johnnie' Johnson, Alan Deere, and Douglas Bader who had been trained at Cranwell, some of whom had flown aircraft with the distinctive red, white, and blue RAF roundel on their machines. Looking out over the wing, to think I was now flying an aircraft with these distinctive and famous markings myself was both an elevating and humbling experience.

Sadly, autumn brought flying on the Chipmunks to a close. We had passed the initial practical phase and we now had to spend the next 18 months in the classroom, learning thermodynamics, principles of flight, navigation, and a host of other technicalities. When not studying, polishing our drill technique on the parade square, or playing sport, we craved desperately to get our hands on the Jet Provost, our next training aircraft.

Throughout their time at Cranwell, the air force would provide opportunities for cadets to expand their skills and absorb new experiences. Soon after I joined the whole of the cadet entry was taken up to the Lake District where we had to climb every peak in the area over two days. It was a tough but rewarding excursion.

Later that year we were flown to Berlin where we spent a few days with the British Army of the Rhine (BAOR) which was responsible for security of the British sector in a partitioned Berlin. They arranged for us to travel into East Berlin through the fabled Checkpoint Charlie where the East German security guards photographed each of us on our passage through the barrier. Entering East Berlin was fascinating but sombre and sobering; it was like being thrust from a universe of light and colour into a sepia monotony.

The following year, instead of departing for my summer leave, I was ordered to report to Portsmouth docks where I would join HMS *Acheron*, a Royal Navy diesel submarine for 14 days. The total crew on board amounted to 100 personnel. My arrival on the boat (submarines in the navy are always referred to as boats) immediately upset the internal balance; I seemed to be in everyone's way.

We sailed out into the Bay of Biscay where we played war games with the navy's surface ships. Some days we were the hunters and others the prey. Pinging Asdic (an early form of sonar used to detect submarines) while on the sea bed followed by depth charges were startlingly real. Diesel-driven, the boat had to breath regularly which meant we had to surface, but where possible the commander would keep it submerged for as long as possible. As a result, carbon dioxide and temperature levels soon rose with a corresponding fall in oxygen, making life in the confined spaces distinctly uncomfortable.

Attack duties were more enjoyable because we would chase destroyers and frigates, firing our torpedoes when in range.

Obviously both the depth charges and torpedoes would inflict no damage to the ship designated for attack.

As I was meant to be on leave enjoying the English summer, such as it was, my heart wasn't in cementing close relations with the navy. Both I and the officers with whom I bunked were relieved when I had to leave prematurely to act as pall bearer at the funeral of one of my squadron entry colleagues who been killed in a car crash.

That winter I was chosen for a trip to the Alps in France where I and about a dozen other cadets revelled in a 10-day rudimentary skiing course with French air force instructors. We had ample opportunity to broaden our horizons while at Cranwell.

To this day I puzzle over my behaviour at the time, trying to rationalise it against my age, my family background, and perhaps my schooling. My parents had recently divorced, which affected me badly. For some obscure yet groundless reason I thought of my fellow trainees as dull and lacking in moral fibre. This latter quality I puzzlingly deemed essential to every fighter pilot, which was my unquestionable destiny, at least in *my* mind. The petty rules of the institution were tedious. Almost involuntarily, I felt obliged to buck the system, leading to disciplinary charges and regular confined-to-barracks penalties or parade square punishment.

All I wanted to do was take to the skies and fly. Luckily, or so I thought at the time, I had a great comrade in arms, Nick Taylor. We finally got to fly the Jet Provost and life changed immeasurably. We were both doing exceptionally well on the advanced stage of the flying course, applying all we had learned in ground school. We had an excellent rapport with our flying instructors. And we both burned with envy watching pilots in their jets taxiing past our classroom windows. We both went solo in the allotted time on the jet. I was ecstatically happy and loving every minute I was in the air flying a jet aircraft, often solo. My destiny was to fly fighters.

In November 1979, without warning, our misdemeanours caught up with us. A cadet from our squadron who had just passed out on completion of his basic training had behaved in a most un-officer like fashion as he went into advanced instruction. The message filtered back that no more students of this calibre were to pass through Cranwell. Nick and I received a summons to appear before the Commandant, Air Vice Marshal Neville Stack, later Sir Neville, who dismissed us from the service and terminated our RAF careers.

My flight instructor at the time of my expulsion went in to bat for me, insisting I was doing well in the course with no signs of future failure, and pleading to have my past ignored.

With the confidence—the arrogance—of youth I thought I had it in the bag. Success and a fabulous future seemed certain. But my dreams and aspirations, as high as the skies I revelled in, lay shattered. It remains the worst day of my life.

Nick was English, and his generous and benevolent parents, Harry and Peggy Taylor, who lived in north London, took me in as a lodger. Harry, a guardsman in his youth, had fought in World War Two and was for a time Montgomery's ADC. The Ministry of Defence, to whom we had both reapplied—firstly to have our expulsions overturned and secondly to be given another chance in the naval air service—turned down my application on both counts.

My bid failed because of my Rhodesian background, and in any case, the political situation had deteriorated further over the past five years. Nick was advised to cool off and reapply. He took the advice, succeeded in his new application, and distinguished himself at the Britannia Royal Naval College, Dartmouth, where he won the Sword of Honour. Sorrowfully, on May 4 1982, he was shot down and killed piloting his Sea Harrier during an attack on Goose Green in the Falklands War. He is buried at Goose Green close to where his aircraft came to rest. Local residents lovingly care for his grave and hold a memorial service for him every year on the anniversary of his death.

It was now early 1970. My mother had moved to Inhassoro in Mozambique with my god parents, Gordon and Norah Brooks, with the idea of setting up a tourist fishing business. Things were not going well, and she needed help. The time came for me to move on too, and reconsider my life and a career in aviation. I knew I had not failed because I couldn't fly, which was my ultimate dream. I packed up and bought a ticket to Lourenco Marques (now Maputo).

Pictured clockwise: 1) Cadet Pilot Officer Ian Rodwell, looking spruce in his Royal Air Force uniform soon after successful admission into RAF Cranwell, May 1968. **2)** Nick Taylor and Lionel Warrington, full of confidence in 1968.

Pictured clockwise: 1) The perks of air force life in 1968. We visit the British Army of the Rhine on inter-service training. Nick Taylor below me shows a keen interest in the tank's interior. 2) Happy day. All my dreams come blissfully true as I make my first solo flight in a Jet Provost, November 26 1969.

CHAPTER EIGHT

My mother and the Belgian Congo coup

While I was at Peterhouse my mother left the private medical sector and joined the government medical service. Many doctors had left after UDI and government medical conditions of service had improved favourably. She was immediately transferred to Kariba, the new town that arose to house the labour force contracted to build the Kariba dam on the Zambezi River which formed the border between Zambia and Rhodesia. The lake that formed behind the Kariba dam wall is still the largest man-made lake by volume in the world. Her move, relatively mundane at the time, would presage dramatic events in our later lives.

During the mid to late 1960s, European colonisers came under pressure to withdraw from their African possessions and grant independence, sometimes leaving instability, or worse, chaos behind. Britain granted independence to Kenya, Northern Rhodesia, which became Zambia; Nyasaland changed to Malawi, and Tanganyika was renamed Tanzania. Belgium pulled out of the Belgian Congo, resulting in a series of bloody civil clashes known as the Congo crisis. The world came to view it as a proxy conflict in the Cold War, with the United States and the then Soviet Union supporting opposing factions.

An intelligent, well-spoken, and respected Moise Tshombe led the autonomous, copper-rich southern Katanga province after the Belgian Congo gained independence in 1960. White Belgians were no longer welcome and fled the country in droves, seeking refuge in countries further south, mainly Northern and Southern Rhodesia. Over the following years civil unrest was rife. To protect himself and, in an effort to vanquish the dreaded Simba rebels, who killed and maimed any who opposed them, Tshombe recruited several hundred international mercenaries. The Simbas received aid from Cuba, under the guidance of Che Guevara and the Russians.

The French sent Tshombe their top soldier of fortune, Colonel Bob Dinard, with his commando, *Les Affreux* (The Dreaded). The British, too, were represented by Colonel 'Mad' Mike Hoare and his entourage of mercenaries, 5 Commando. Throughout the hostilities, Rhodesian pilot and businessman, Captain Jack Malloch, regularly flew arms and personnel into the country and in the process became good friends with Tshombe, who in the end gave Malloch his personal four-engine DC-4 aircraft. In the process, Malloch also became close to both Bob Dinard and Mike Hoare. The civil war in the Congo raged for several years during the 1960s with Tshombe being ousted and forced into exile, then instated as president of the whole of the Congo, only to be deposed again and driven back into exile.

Under such extraordinary conditions the situation was ripe for the introduction of mercenaries such as Hoare and Dinard and their men. General Mobutu had seized power and installed himself as the president of the Congo in 1967. A plot was hatched to stage a coup and reinstate Tshombe as president. According to Wikipedia, in 1967 the Congolese authorities sentenced Tshombe to death *in absentia*. On June 30 of that year, Tshombe, in a bid to stage a coup, attempted a return to Africa in a British-piloted Hawker Siddley aircraft, but a

French intelligence agent forced its diversion to Algiers where Tshombe was subsequently imprisoned. A legal battle took place between the Congolese, seeking his extradition, and Western supporters calling for his release. The Algerians resisted both demands. The plans for the coup were too far advanced to abandon, and the prevailing view was that if the coup was successful, recovering Tshombe from Algeria would be possible.

Fierce fighting broke out throughout the Congo with Jack Malloch heavily involved, including a hot extraction rescuing civilians and soldiers out of a small airfield. One of the mercenaries remained behind to give covering fire as the aircraft took off. Realising he would not make it onto the taxiing plane, he pleaded with his colleagues on board to shoot him, having run out of ammunition., which they did to save him being hacked to death by the swarming Simba, the fate his corpse suffered minutes later.

It was a dramatic rescue which provided the foundation for a novel called *The Wild Geese,* loosely based on fact and written soon after by a Rhodesian lawyer, Daniel Carney. It also became a famous Hollywood movie of the same name starring Richard Burton, Richard Harris, and Roger Moore.

Meanwhile, in the ensuing melee in Kisangani, Dinard had been shot in the head and captured and was due to be flown to Kinshasa as a prize for the president, Colonel Mobutu. However, once aboard the aircraft, one of Dinard's soldiers, Jean-Louis Domange, took control and persuaded the pilots to fly to Rhodesia where at least Dinard would not face imprisonment if he recovered. In doing so, Domange became one of the world's first hijackers, but his actions no doubt saved many lives. In later times we would see much of Domange when he became our station manager in Libreville.

The aircraft ran short of fuel and just managed to land at Kariba airport, as depicted in the novel. My mother received a call in the early hours of the morning to alert her to the imminent arrival of an aircraft with many wounded on board. She was able to tend to the injured , including Dinard, whose condition she stabilised before commandeering a Rhodesian Air Force helicopter and pilot. They flew him directly to Salisbury General Hospital where Professor Laurence Levy, one of the top neurosurgeons in the world at the time, operated on him to remove the bullet, allowing Dinard to make a full recovery. My mother was sworn to secrecy for her part in saving Dinard's life, probably more for her own protection, and only told me the story many years later.

Dinard went on to help stage several coups in west Africa and the Comoros Islands over subsequent years and is generally regarded as France's most famous (or infamous) mercenary. Throughout his subsequent career, he remained in continual contact with his long-time colleague, Jack Malloch.

CHAPTER NINE

Seeding the clouds— Rhodesia and the early flying years—1970 to 1974

I spent a couple of long months in Inhassoro, with little action to report. Mozambique, a Portuguese colony, was steeped in bureaucracy and permits had not been issued for the fishing boats which were rusting at anchor. My mother became infatuated with a one-legged World War Two veteran who ran the local hotel. She decided to accept his offer to return to Salisbury (Harare), but the relationship failed to mature because he already had a partner, much younger than her. He became manager of the Salisbury Sports Club and let her use the manager's flat until she found alternative accommodation. In the meantime, I had joined her and started the process of renewing my flying career, while she worked as a doctor in Accident and Emergencies (A&E) at the Salisbury General Hospital.

As a result of some messy inter-family financial arrangements, my grandfather funded my commercial pilot's license course at a cost of £3,500 at Mount Hampden (now Charles Prince) airport about 15 miles east of Salisbury. The course was well attended and very professionally run. Most students passed on schedule. By this time, I had met Jennifer Barstow, who I married soon after, adopting her four year old son, Dominic, in the process. We lived in a very small cottage well out of town in the suburb of Edenvale.

Times were not easy and money was tight, but I was extremely fortunate to be offered a job as instructor/charter pilot by Skywork, the company with which I had just completed my training. Sam, my son, was born in 1971, and we found a house in Avondale which saved the long journey I previously had to take from the west of the city. Life was good, I was busy flying and building up valuable experience towards the 1,000 hours of piloting time as the threshold for moving up in the aviation world. Nicholas, my second son, was born in 1973, by which time the Rhodesian Department of Civil Aviation accepted me as an operations officer (commonly known as a flight operations inspector today). It was an interesting job. My basic roles were to set and mark exam papers for the private pilot's license (PPL), aircraft type conversion exams, the testing of pilots qualifying for their PPL, and doing test flights on different aircraft types that needed a Certificate of Airworthiness (C of A) renewal test flight. Consequently, my repertoire of aircraft flown increased significantly.

By 1974 I was flying an average of 15 different aircraft types a month which involved as many as 20 different types of tests on pilots. I was also lucky to be sent on a multi-engine instructor's course which I thoroughly enjoyed, and which stood me in good stead for my future instructional career.

Another of my airborne tasks involved cloud seeding. The meteorological department in conjunction with the agricultural ministry wanted to ascertain the benefits of seeding growing cumulonimbus clouds with dust particles to encourage the onset of rain. The country had recently experienced a couple of years of drought resulting in poor agricultural yields. The authorities believed there was merit in seeding the clouds that often dissipated before providing the much-needed rain. The Rhodesian Air Force had already embarked upon a cloud seeding programme using the Douglas DC-3. The Department of Civil Aviation had a turbocharged Cessna 320 aircraft which it would use as the research aircraft. A small porthole was fitted through one of the passenger doors through which a Very cartridge full of dust particles could be fired into the cloud at the correct moment.

Scientists involved thought at the time there were not enough particles present in the average growing cloud to convert the moist air into raindrops with the result that the cloud would quickly evaporate. By providing the cloud with enough minute solid particles the water vapour would have a vehicle onto which to form a water droplet, which would then grow and eventually fall as rain. Engineers also fitted the aircraft with a funnelled scoop in the roof with which to trap and measure the amount of rain produced.

Dicky Dives and I were the two pilots chosen to fly the research aircraft. On a day when cumulus clouds began to form, we would climb to between 16,000 and 21,000 feet so that we could enter the cloud at about a quarter of its total height from the top. By this time, we would fly totally on instruments, enduring the associated turbulence such conditions caused. As the aircraft experienced a large updraft the researcher would fire off one or more cartridges into the cloud. At times the turbulence was so severe we would look back to see the researcher and his assistant pinned to the roof only to tumble back to the floor when we hit the next up draft.

On many occasions the turbocharger for the engines would ice up and the engines would stop either singly, causing some asymmetry, or together giving rise to an eery silence except for the noise of the air rushing past us. Once out of the cloud and back in clear air we would restart the engines relatively easily. Often the windscreens iced up completely leading us to think we were still in cloud until we looked out of the side window to see we were back in the clear. Once we had seeded the cloud and could see that it was producing rain, we now had to descend to between 2,000 feet and 3,000 feet and fly through the cloud twice, the second pass at 90 degrees to the first. By now the base of cloud was sometimes several miles across and seriously dark; at times it seemed like flying into thick chocolate. The funnel contraption would now collect the rain which the researchers would collect in a tin beaker and measure. Pilots do not enjoy experiencing the levels of turbulence we used to encounter during this project. I confess I was relieved when the cloud seeding research project came to an end.

The highlight of that year for me, however, was a conversion onto the DC-3 Douglas Dakota, or Dak as it was affectionately known, with the national airline, Air Rhodesia. It was a formidable aircraft and an absolute delight to fly. Through a government loan scheme available to civil servants I bought a brand-new Renault 4. Life was improving further.

The flying was interesting, challenging, and rewarding all at the same time. My colleagues as operations officers were two former wartime pilots, Phil Palmer and Tony Birch, from whom I learnt so much. Birch used to set the commercial pilot licence (CPL) exams and Palmer the airline transport pilot licence (ATPL) tests. Candidates sat the professional exams every six months. We would put in weeks of preparation to ensure their veracity, accuracy, and fairness. Each of us would sit the exams prior to their approval to ensure we met the above criteria.

I was able to get a reasonable amount of experience on the DC-3 as every registered aircraft of the type in the country had to have an annual C of A test flight which I was scheduled to undertake. This was daunting as some of the airlines had highly experienced DC-3 pilots who would have to accompany this young blond-haired boy as their co-pilot. Luckily, I soon gained a reputation for competency and won approval from these old hands.

Twice a month I had to take the government aircraft, a Cessna 206, down to Bulawayo to supervise PPL and CPL flight tests there. To the dismay of anyone accompanying me I would wait until dark before returning to Salisbury because to qualify for my ATPL I had to complete 100 hours of night cross country flying. To them, flying for two hours in a single engine aircraft in darkness was a long way from their idea of fun. It was always a relief to see the lights of Salisbury emerge out of the inky blackness because our plane struggled to pick up the available navigation aids.

Another of my tasks as an FOI was aircraft accident investigations, which again was fascinating but time consuming. If an aircraft was involved in accident, we had to be the first on the scene, once emergency services had rescued the injured or recovered any dead bodies from in the crash. We had a team of accident investigators involving operations, engineering, and any other related discipline as required. I attended an accident investigation course and assisted at a few incidents before I became head of operations. The process was meticulous in establishing the cause of the accident and we spent hours analysing and investigating both the aircraft as well as the pilot's actions prior to the event. Sadly, on too many occasions the pilots were no longer alive to give more insight into events leading up to the crash. The reports were minutely detailed and took much time to write prior to approval for public release by the director.

The worst accident investigation in which I assisted was that of a four engine DC-4 operated by Wenela from Francistown (Botswana) which had been refuelled with A1 jet fuel instead of the standard octane fuel used by large piston engine aircraft. The engines on take-off were unable to generate the required power to get airborne and the aircraft crashed into trees, exploding, and killing more than 60 of the people on board, including the crew.

Accident investigation is essentially detective work; you have to examine all the evidence to establish a cause. Our skills were particularly tested on one occasion when a light aircraft spun into the ground in the local Bulawayo flying area, killing both occupants. The young pilot had recently gained his PPL and had taken his father up for a flip. His father had never flown before and sadly for both of them the lad decided to show off his skills by doing a spin.

Pilots should never undertake a spin intentionally. It was only on the syllabus to demonstrate how to recover if ever the aircraft was flown badly enough to cause it to spin, a stalled condition all about axis where the forward speed is virtually zero, but the rate of descent is extreme. The operations engineering officer (OEO), John Pienaar, and I were the lead investigators. We came to the conclusion, based on the post mortem findings, that his son had lost control of the aircraft. As a result, the father was so startled that he grabbed hold of the controls and would not release them. In desperation, the son had tried to force his father to release the controls, hitting him about the head repeatedly. The father showed contusions to his face which were not as a result of the aircraft crashing. We found the finding humbling and sad.

By 1974 I had gained more experience and had qualified for my ATPL as well as doing a fair amount of flying on the civilian version of the DC-3. The Rhodesian Air Force was now busy because the so-called liberation war, or second chimurenga, had ramped up. To supplement the regular air force pilots the military qualified a number of civilian pilots who formed the Volunteer Reserve (VR). The basic requirements for acceptance into the VR were that you had pre-viously been a qualified military pilot, had passed your interview with the Officer Commanding 3 Squadron and the OC of the Volunteer Reserve, and had then subsequently passed your induction training on the DC-3/C-47 Dakota. At that stage VR pilots only flew as part of 3 Squadron which contained the C-47. (The C-47 is the military variant of the DC-3 with a cargo door and strengthened floor).

I had been vetted by a couple of the VR pilots as I was very keen to join and make my contribution as an active pilot rather than performing a mundane ground job during my callups. By now, all able-bodied males in the country had to commit to some sort of military role on a regular basis. The stumbling block was that as I had not actually qualified as a military pilot by obtaining my wings, it was deemed impossible for me to join the VR.

One evening, a Mt Hampden airport cocktail party featured some of the hierarchy of the Rhodesian Air Force (RhAF), including the then head of the service, Air Marshal Mick McLaren. I learned he had attended the same induction course as my brother, Tony. When I was finally introduced to him, I mentioned Tony's name and immediately McLaren wanted to know more. I gave him a brief history, adding I had written to him personally requesting that I join the VR but had received a standard 'thanks but no thanks' response from the officer commanding. He suggested I give it some time and that I would hear from the air force in due course. Sure enough, a few days later I received a letter asking me to attend an interview with Group Captain Ossie Penton, OCVR among other roles. We got on well and I soon found myself in an interview with Squadron Leader George Alexander DFC, head of 3 Squadron. To become a fully qualified VR pilot, I would have to pass all the ATPL subjects, pass all the flying tests to qualify me to fly the military DC-3 (C-47) and then, when I attained my command on the aircraft I would, only then receive my flying badge (military wings) and become a fully-fledged member of 3 Squadron and the VR.

I joined 3 Squadron late in 1974 and step by step completed each requirement. Passing the ATPL subjects was relatively straightforward since only recently I had sat them for my civil licence. As the only 'unqualified' military pilot on the squadron it took some time for the regulars to accept me. They regarded this unqualified civilian with some scepticism. However, it was easy for me to be humble in their venerated company as they were all experienced, professional, and well qualified as well as thoroughly likeable.

Conveniently, I was already competent on the aircraft type, but this time, with more maturity, I enjoyed the rigorous air force discipline. This applied especially to the standard operating procedures (SOPs) adopted by the squadron, so that regardless of who you flew with, the procedures, checklists, and call outs were identical, with no room for personal interpretation. By the end of November, I had completed all the necessary exercises, passed my basic green card instrument flying rating and night flying, and was now considered operational in a co-pilot role.

The flying was varied. On a regular basis we performed a bus service, replenishing the various forward airfields (FAFs) with provisions, personnel, and weaponry. To deliver the message to terrorists to give themselves up we often flew Sky Shout missions where the aircraft was fitted with a large speaker in the doorway blaring out a message in several local languages. We would circle over areas known to contain groups of terrorists and with the engines throttled right back to minimum power, the message reached the ground loud and clear. Apparently, it had a most unsettling effect on those concerned, especially on a dark night. Although an important part of the war effort, we pilots thought it a task to avoid. Flying around in circles for between six and eight hours at night was boring, although we occasionally saw and heard small arms fire directed at us. But with nothing substantial to aim at other than disembodied noise, the results were negligible.

One crew each day would operate the early morning para detail. The parachute training section never stopped preparing and qualifying soldiers as paratroops. Initially most of the training involved the Special Air Service (SAS) but as the war progressed the majority of troops, from the Rhodesia Light Infantry (RLI), the Rhodesian African Rifles (RAR), and the Selous Scouts were all parachute trained. Each of us on the squadron, despite getting up well before dawn, enjoyed the early morning para details which involved dropping sticks, or small groups of trainee parachutists. We would fly at low altitude where they would jump via a static line which would deploy their chutes without them having to do so manually. Often, we would then climb to at least 13,000 feet to deploy the free fall parachutists, as well as all the instructors, who loved this aspect of their job. We pilots would control the drop by warning the dispatchers in the back with the signal of 'red light on'. All would ready themselves in the doorway of the aircraft waiting for the signal 'green light on' which was their cue to jump, or be pushed out of the aircraft if they were at all reluctant.

The idea was to drop the parachutists within the confines of the airport perimeter which enabled a simple recovery back to the training hangar. We relied heavily on the windsock which was conveniently located in the drop zone to help us calculate how much of a lay off angle to use before we signalled them to jump. If the wind was calm the process was simple: we would drop them in line with the windsock allowing for the speed of the aircraft to drift them accurately into their drop zone. As the wind became stronger, making the necessary allowance for drift became more complex and on occasion the upper wind at exit level would be substantially different from the wind on the ground. As a result, the trainees would land some distance from their intended touchdown requiring a long walk with all their kit and chute back to base. It made us less popular than we felt we deserved.

Later in the conflict, when dropping into operational situations, we would ask a helicopter to throw out a smoke flare which would give us the information we needed to measure the drift and lay off we should allow for. Accuracy of drops under those circumstances became time and operationally critical. A bonus to the early morning para detail was a free, hot breakfast in the mess once back on the ground.

We also used the aircraft as an ambulance, a hearse, and much later as a gunship with a .303 Browning machine gun mounted in the doorway. Such was the nature of my flying on 3 Squadron for a time. This would change considerably in the subsequent months and years as the bush war intensified.

CHAPTER 10

My father the spy, and early war games

Much time has elapsed, and the world and attitudes and perceptions have changed. In the 1960s, however, the world was mostly politically stable except for the United States' involvement in Vietnam. In 1965, when Rhodesia declared its independence from British rule, the mother country was furious that its so-called favourite African child had decided to govern alone. Britain was determined to bring Rhodesia to its knees economically because its political and military influence had continued to wane after the exhausting impact of the Second World War.

It imposed sanctions on Rhodesia with the support of the United Nations and countries sympathetic to the British cause, of which there were many, as the United Kingdom was still regarded in theory as a leading nation. The supply of fuel was suspended, but luckily some countries such as Greece and Portugal were sympathetic to Rhodesia and fuel was shipped in from Greek ships via the Mozambican (Portuguese colony) port of Beira. Eventually fuel was supplied by South Africa who saw an opportunity that by assisting Rhodesia they could possibly delay a similar fate by a decade, which they achieved.

At the same time both Russia and China recognised the long-term benefit and gains to be had assisting black opposition leaders in their struggle for independence. This they achieved not by political means but through the barrel of a gun. In the earlier years, all who left the country to fight for independence were sent to Russia or China to be trained in guerrilla warfare. Later they were trained either in Zambia or Mozambique when the numbers became too great to transport them to overseas destinations.

The strategy was that, once trained they would infiltrate back into the country and kill and maim indiscriminately, causing terror and instability. This they achieved.

The Soviets never benefited greatly from their involvement when, just over a decade after Zimbabwe's independence, the USSR dissolved. China, however, played the long game. Once their African nationalist clients gained power, they called in their debt. It took, and continues to take, the form of minerals, timber, coal, food, and other commodities, as well as gaining access to strategic sites, facilities, and contracts for major infrastructure projects.

A spin-off of the British connection was that Rhodesia's armed forces were extremely well trained. C Squadron Special Air Service (SAS), the Rhodesian division, had fought alongside the British forces in successfully quelling the communist terrorist threat in Malaysia and as a consequence, many of the senior members of the armed forces had direct experience in combatting guerrilla warfare.

Soon after it became independent, Zambia provided the terrorists sanctuary as well as a springboard for entry into Rhodesia. Before the war started in earnest, although isolated attacks on farmsteads within the country had already begun, the Rhodesian intelligence services wanted as much information as they could glean from inside Zambia.

In August 1966, my father, while on a visit to my mother in Kamativi, was called on by two members of the Rhodesian Special Branch police. They asked him to provide them with as much information as he could on the locations of guerrilla camps and numbers of personnel. Since he had a small aeroplane, they felt he was an ideal candidate. He was subsequently briefed, as I would learn only years later, by members of the Rhodesian SAS. They asked him to undertake many missions which he documented and diarised himself. It involved driving all over the country as well as flying from place to place to photograph any suspected camps from the air. Still at school, I was oblivious to all of this. Others were on a strictly need-to-know foundation.

When I turned 17, I went on holiday to Zambia for a stint on the farm. As I was now of driving age I went into Livingstone, our local town, completed my driving test, and gained my licence which I still possess to this day.

By now more and more terrorist incursions and attacks from Zambia-based combatants were taking place within Rhodesia. I discovered my father had already helped the SAS in some clandestine operations which had ended in failure through mediocre planning and execution. The first involved members of the SAS being flown into Lusaka in the middle of the night. My father was to meet them and guide them to their target which they would blow up. Although he rendezvoused with them and led them to the destination it became clear they could not destroy the selected building without a high risk of detection. They aborted the exercise and he ferried them back to the airport where the same aircraft from their inward flight collected them and flew them back to Rhodesia.

The second incident proved more serious. A team of SAS and a Special Branch policeman were to boat across the Zambezi below the Chirundu bridge with a considerable quantity of explosives with which they intended to blow up a terrorist barrack block. My father was to wait in the hills on the Zambian side of the river. On receiving their signal he would drive down to the river and transport them to their target, returning them once the mission was accomplished. He was patiently waiting at the allocated time when he heard and saw a massive explosion on the Rhodesian bank. He waited until just before dawn and when no signal came, he left, ignorant of events. He found out only much later when he next met his SAS minders that inexplicably a detonator had self-activated, causing a massive explosion and killing three of the SAS team as well as the SB policeman.

Sending teams of special forces into the country so far had failed, so they devised a scheme where my father could operate on his own. He met his handlers in Rhodesia who coached him through a quick explosives course and gave him a 'bomb' which he would use to blow up a target of their choice in due course. A menu of options presented itself ranging from Government House where President Kenneth Kaunda lived, to government buildings, or even the airport. The rationale was that the bomb was to induce fear among the locals but not to take life. Eventually he received a coded radio message transmitted from the Rhodesia Broadcasting Corporation (RBC) in August 1966. It replicated the method by which Allied agents in France during World War Two received messages over the wireless from the BBC, making an apparently innocent reference to weather conditions, or similar. The target was the fuel dump at the entry to Lusaka airport.

My father was very wary. As a security precaution, he had received advice against soliciting help from any of his farming colleagues. Since the *modus operandi* of his mission was a drive-by bombing, he couldn't steer and deploy the explosive device at the same time. Who better to trust than his loyal son?

We were chatting at home one evening when he told me what he had been doing to help the Rhodesian security forces, and gave me details of his next task. Would I help him? I felt honoured and privileged to be asked. At an age where I had read many accounts of the escalating war, it seemed natural—even exciting—to be invited to join the action. The next day we drove up to Lusaka in two vehicles, he in the Land Rover and me in a Ford Cortina which he had recently bought. We used two cars as a precaution in case something went wrong, allowing us to split up and make our own way out of the country.

We checked in to the Blue Boar Inn and the next day conducted a recce of the airport, planning our mission which we would carry out that night. The next day we would depart and go back home. The Land Rover was a single cab truck version. You could cover the tray of the vehicle with a canopy or have it open. We had fitted the canopy before leaving the farm and had made a set of false number plates which we attached just before we left the hotel. His handlers had briefed him that he must prime the device before dispatch otherwise it would fail to detonate. We drove to a quiet lane close to the airport and parked to prime the bomb. I would position myself in the back and he would drive down the approach road into the airport with the fuel dump on our left. At the appropriate moment he would shout 'go' and I would hurl the explosive device over the fence into the fuel dump.

This was the first flaw in our plan. The explosives had a 60 minute time delay between priming and detonation, allowing us a margin to make our escape. We sat in the front of the car and a long discussion followed as to who would actually arm the thing. To me it looked like something from a Heath Robinson cartoon. It was a parcel, slightly smaller than a brick. To prepare it for detonation, you had to pull the two visible pins out of the casing. By now, my father was visibly agitated. I think the folly of involving his only son on a dangerous and potentially fatal escapade had suddenly dawned on him. Besides, based on previous history, the integrity of the device was probably suspect. He was sweating profusely and I suspect he was on the point of abandoning the mission, when I, too naive to know better, pulled the pins out.

Mercifully, there was no explosion. We were still alive, but now we had to get going as we had little time before the device would go off. I jumped in the back with the package and undid the back canopy so that I could do a backhand throw and off we went. He turned into the approach road to the airport and after some time I could see the fuel dump just over the fence. On his shout I threw the parcel as hard as I could and saw it sail over the fence into the fuel dump—hundreds of fuel drums stacked together. The SAS had assured my father that the time delay would work, allowing us to escape well clear of the airport before mayhem broke loose.

Wrong. The bomb detonated on impact producing a colossal explosion and an even larger fireball. We now had no option but to drive into the airport arrival area, turn around and drive back past the fire. People were shouting, running in all directions, and blowing whistles. Dad panicked and accelerated furiously, attracting an unhealthy amount of unwanted attention. We shot down the road and turned in the opposite direction to the one we should have taken. He drove around the suburbs for a short while before stopping and letting me into the front, but not before we removed the false registration plates.

We heard police vehicles and fire engines rushing to the airport, but elsewhere all seemed calm, so we drove back to the hotel. My father was clearly stressed, so I tried to burn and flush away the false number plates, finally resorting to stashing their charred remains in the toilet cistern. At the same time I attempted to persuade him to get some sleep which for both of us failed to come easily.

On analysis we should have driven into the airport arrival area, turned around, and thrown the device as we were leaving the airport, not entering it. Bless hindsight.

I awoke very early the next morning and left in the Cortina just as dawn was breaking. I drove all day and crossed the Victoria Falls bridge in the early afternoon. As I crossed the bridge over the Deka River, my mother was waiting for me. She was aware of what was going on. In the past she would regularly go down to the bridge on the road from Dett (now Dete) to Kamativi to wait for my father to arrive from his trips away. She had heard the news of the bombing on the radio and was worried sick, not having learned of our fate.

My father had to maintain a business-as-usual facade and returned to the farm, arriving in Kamativi some days later. He was mortified that he had put me in such danger, but being young, I had already put it behind me. However, my interest in an involvement in further war games seemed to dissolve. I never told a soul about my escapade, especially when I went back to school the following term, and kept my secret for decades. I am also sure my father kept parts of the story from his SAS handlers. They would have felt embarrassed that the mission had very nearly gone horribly wrong, and furious at our muddled thinking.

CHAPTER 11

Flights for life—1975

In 1975, 10 years after my father's and my counter-terror adventure in Zambia, I was once again involved in the war, and on a more serious note, flying with 3 Squadron.

What follows is an account of what I experienced and witnessed during the war years. Hundreds of other pilots, many much braver and more experienced than me, have their own experiences and war stories to tell. However, I have now heard and read too many exaggerated or even false tales based on historical events and others' exploits to boost the narrators' egos or reputations. So many contributed to the successes and failures of the war years. I believe it is important for me to tell my story and not anyone else's.

It is also pertinent that we on the squadron were tasked and briefed on a need-to-know basis. Security, often amounting to blanket secrecy, was paramount and consequently the fewer people who knew what the security forces were up to the better. As a result, we only discovered after the event what operations or battles others had been involved in, even though we were often central to the action.

It is also equally important to understand that on 3 Squadron, most of the time we never knew who the soldiers were in the back of the aircraft. However, from time to time on important operational sorties, the soldier in command would brief us. As a result we came to know particular personalities if they happened to fly with us on more than one occasion. I met few of the brave soldiers that I dropped out of the back of my aircraft, but I was privileged to operate with one particular hero on many an operation. Captain, later Major Grahame Wilson, went on to become Rhodesia's mostly highly decorated soldier, and head of the respected and feared C Squadron Rhodesian Special Air Services (SAS). His and his elite unit's daring and courage under always taxing conditions became legend.

It would be helpful at this stage to explain a little of the operational prosecution of the bush war from Rhodesia's perspective.

The country was divided up into six operational areas each with a Joint Operational Centre (JOC) and each had one or more forward airfields (FAFs) which were the main operational headquarters for that area. Operation Hurricane was situated in the north east of the country with FAF 2 (Kariba), 3 (Centenary), 4 (Mount Darwin) and 5 (Mtoko) respectively. The main base of New Sarum (Salisbury Airport) head-quartered Squadrons 3 (Dakotas), 5 (Canberras), 7 (Alouettes), and 8 (Bells).

Operation Thrasher in the east of the country had FAF 8 (Grand Reef/Umtali) and 6 (Chipinga). Operation Repulse in the south east had FAF 7 (Buffalo Range/Chiredzi) and 9 (Rutenga). Operation Tangent in the west had FAF 1 (Wankie) and 10 (Gwanda). The fifth area, Operation Grapple, was in the middle of the country served by the main air force base, Thornhill, where Squadron 1 (Hunters) and 4 (Provosts/Lynxes/Trojans) were based. A sixth, Operation Splinter, covered the northwest—Lake Kariba and parts of the Zambezi River and valley downstream.

Through most of 1975 I was largely involved in resupply flights to the various FAFs and other operational airfields, mainly in the Operation Hurricane area. We carried out regular shuttle services between the main airfields, changing over personnel as well as resupplying.

My first active exposure to the conflict came early in March when Noel Vonhoff and I were on a regular resupply run to the north east of the country. It was fairly late in the afternoon when we were directed to fly immediately to an airstrip in the Mana Pools area in the Zambezi Valley instead of returning directly to New Sarum. A detachment of the SAS had been ambushed, sustaining several casualties.

M.A.S.H, a great film, had recently been a hit in the cinemas, resulting in a successful television series of the same name, then airing on Rhodesian Television (RTV). It was mostly light-hearted, set during the Korean War and examining the lives of the doctors, nurses, and the wounded in an operational field hospital. But it also occasionally touched on the physical, emotional, and psychological damage war inflicts on its participants.

Landing at the strip was like visiting the set of M.A.S.H. Dust flew everywhere with the arrival of helicopters and their cargo of wounded soldiers. Blood- and dust-caked troops deplaning from the choppers had gaunt, battle-weary faces etched deeply with post contact stress. Many were wounded, some seriously. Time was critical in loading the injured onto the aircraft so we could casevac (casualty evacuate) them urgently to Salisbury. One of the wounded, a cockney, had been shot in the leg and stomach and was in great and very vocal pain. Another, Trooper 'Rocky' Walton, just 20 years of age, was critically wounded and was having trouble breathing.

There were too few medics on board to treat all the wounded at the same time. They asked if one of we pilots could come back to help. Noel left me to fly the aircraft and went to help tend Trooper Walton who, though severely injured, could still converse lucidly with him.

I faced a difficult dilemma. We had to climb out of the Zambezi Valley where the altitude is relatively low at about 1,000 feet above sea level. The troops would have acclimatised to the higher oxygen levels. We now had to climb to between 6,000 and 7,000 feet above sea level to get safely to Salisbury, a high-altitude airfield at nearly 5,000 feet. Additionally, the low-level turbulence was considerable, consistent with the time of day and year and made worse by my flying as fast as I could.

I decided that Walton's need for oxygen outweighed any discomfort the other wounded and the medics might feel from the low altitude turbulence. Darkness had now fallen, but once we were over the Zambezi escarpment conditions smoothed out. However, I was still flying at maximum speed and minimum altitude to maintain optimum oxygen levels. Lack of height made contacting Salisbury difficult on the VHF radio. I eventually managed to get a relay through another aircraft, declaring a medical emergency and requesting a straight-in approach to the non-standard runway 24.

Flying in and out of Salisbury, 99 per cent of the time we would use runway 06 but tonight it would take too long to set up a standard landing on that strip. Noel sent me a message: he was giving mouth -to-mouth resuscitation to the soldier to help him breath, but his life hung in the balance. Could I fly any faster? I could not coax another knot out of the Dak. After an apparent eternity, we were close enough to Salisbury to communicate directly with the airport tower. The controllers gave me a heading to steer so that I would intercept the final approach track at about 5,200 feet which would be sufficient for the fastest possible time to land.

With Noel committed to his life-and-death struggle in the back, my solo landing would be more difficult. The DC-3 has a much more complex system of adjusting flaps and lowering and locking the undercarriage than other aircraft. Performing extra procedures while still manning the controls was doubly tricky. Fortunately, nothing went awry, and we landed and taxied to the apron where emergency medical teams were standing by to race the wounded to the Andrew Fleming Hospital. Noel had done a fantastic job trying to keep his patient alive, effectively breathing for him. His efforts led to extensive bruising on his lips and mouth.

We air force personnel, especially on 3 Squadron, were lucky in at least one regard: the aircraft always had to return to base overnight. And base always included a bar, so we were able to finish a challenging day in the mess with a few drinks to help damp down the adrenalin before going home. The poor troops we had left in the valley had no such luxury.

On my way home I stopped at the hospital to ask after the welfare of the wounded. Initially the nurse would not give me any details because as yet contact with the next of kin had not been completed. When I explained who I was and what we had gone through to get them to hospital, she relented, telling me that sadly the young man Noel had tried so valiantly to save was pronounced dead on arrival. It was a moment of great sadness; he was a fine-looking youngster with so much life ahead of him. His death was also puzzlingly surreal. Initially we were more worried about the cockney soldier who appeared to be more seriously wounded than Trooper Walton. Apparently, a contributory factor to his death was a large dose of morphine in the field and another aboard the aircraft which made breathing difficult. I do not suggest for a moment any form of negligence. This, after all, was war where disaster calls for desperate measures.

A couple of days later I returned to the hospital and visited the cockney soldier. Although saddened by the death of his colleague, he seemed in high spirits and good humour, and appeared eager, once mended, to re-join his unit.

Air Trans Africa and the legendary Jack Malloch

Earlier in the year I had cause to visit the offices of Air Trans Africa (ATA), a cargo airline run by the legendary Captain Jack Malloch, of whom much has been written elsewhere. A Rhodesian, he volunteered for the RAF during World War Two and flew Spitfires on the same squadron as Ian Smith. Smith would later, as Prime Minister of

Rhodesia, lead his country into a unilateral declaration of independence from Britain and a subsequent bush war. Malloch was shot down over Italy but rescued and sheltered by partisans who helped him escape to freedom and to re-join his squadron. After the war, he returned to Rhodesia and founded several airlines, becoming involved in gunrunning operations during the Congo troubles and the Biafran war. Readers interested in this maverick of aviation will find ample reward in Alan Brough's book *Jack Malloch: Legend of the African Skies.*

I bumped into ATA's chief pilot, Colin Miller, an old friend of Tony, my brother. ATA operated two DC-7(F) aircraft. The DC-7 was the last major piston-engine aircraft the Douglas Aircraft Corporation built and I was fortunate enough during my time with the DCA to have flown to Libreville (Gabon) and back as an observer. I found it a fascinating experience because the DC-7's engines were probably the most complex four piston units to operate.

Colin informed me that the company was about to purchase a Lockheed Electra which was a large four engine turbo propeller aircraft. It was faster than the DC-7 and could carry a greater cargo load. He indicated that ATA was looking to hire more pilots to crew the Electra and asked if I was interested. Without a moment's hesitation I told him I was. I felt I had come to a crossroad in my aviation career and, while my job in the DCA was multifaceted and absorbing, it was time to obtain experience on larger aircraft. I added that I would be even more excited with an offer of a job on the DC-8 if there was ever a vacancy or demand. Although ATA did not then possess the aircraft, I knew from my position in the DCA that a number of ATA pilots were in the US undergoing a DC-8 conversion course. The information was top secret at the time.

From April to August I flew about 50 hours a month evenly spread between air force commitments and the everyday Department of Civil Aviation flight tests and checks.

In late July a call came through from Group Captain Jack Blanchard-Simms, the Operations Manager of ATA, offering me a job as a first officer on the DC-8 starting late August with a course in Amsterdam run by KLM airlines. My joy and excitement were intense, and I had no qualms about tendering my resignation to the DCA. There was a problem in that my contract as a government employee insisted on three-months' notice. Ian Berry, the then director and I had a good relationship and after a lengthy discussion he reluctantly released me from the terms of my contract.

In the late evening of August 29, nine of us climbed into the back of the DC-8, TR-LVK, and were flown to Amsterdam via Libreville. We checked into the Frommer Hotel at Schiphol airport which was to be our home for the next seven weeks. Six of us were pilots and three were flight engineers. We were all new to Air Gabon Cargo, now our employer, except for the two flight engineers, Ken de Goveia and John Borejzso, who previously flew on the ATA DC-7. KLM, the Dutch national airline, ran the DC-8 course. None of us dared question the political implications of our being trained in Europe despite the sanctions imposed against Rhodesia, which included travel bans on Rhodesian passport-holders. Fortunately, as aircrew we could use our crew identity cards and bypass immigration authorities. As far as our Dutch hosts were concerned, a Gabonese company employed us and we presumably lived in that country. We were briefed at great length before we left as to how we were to behave and never to allude to the fact we were from Rhodesia.

For a time it was a bizarre existence. Often the KLM instructors would quiz us curiously on life in Gabon and why we spoke no French since that was the national language. After a while they wised up and stopped asking questions. In the meantime we could not phone home or receive calls from Salisbury. Our safest form of communication was to write letters and send them through the company mailbag or give them to crew members who were flying in and out. And still, none of us had ever flown a large four engine jet before although some had flown jet trainers in the military and others had flown the four-engine Viscount with Air Rhodesia.

Once we had qualified on the aircraft, we were issued with Gabonese pilot licenses which were renewed every six months in accordance with standard aviation practice. I still have my *Republique Gabonaise, Licence de Pilote de Ligne, numero 143*. We all passed the necessary ground school exams and progressed to the simulator training program. We were divided into three crews; I was paired with Mike Smith and we were trained by a personable young KLM training first officer, Adrian de Ras.

At the end of the course and after graduation, he said that during the first simulator session he had never seen such poor procedural performances, but had also never witnessed two pilots raise their game so significantly. He believed we had improved to such an extent that both of us demonstrated the necessary skills for entry into KLM as a pilot. High praise indeed. Adrian later rose to the rank of fleet manager on a KLM fleet which was to be expected; he was in every respect a class act. Our last simulator session was a check ride with another KLM examiner who was fully satisfied with our performance. We had now passed the simulator phase of our course.

Sam Richman had also passed that morning. He, Mike, and I decided to celebrate with a visit to central Amsterdam to enjoy a few beers which had been in short supply since the beginning of the course. We were all tired and decided to pull out of the merriment relatively early, boarding the waiting bus back to Schiphol airport and our hotel.

Unfortunately, the transport ran only once an hour and we had just missed the previous bus. We all fell asleep and woke to the bus moving through the suburbs of Amsterdam. As I stirred, I found Mike standing on the seat next to me, having opened the sliding roof hatch. He was enjoying the cool breeze after the stifling temperatures from the bus's heaters. I joined him and we enjoyed our view of the passing countryside and small towns. To get a better look and more air, we stood on the back-rest of the seat. I felt comfortable lying with the top half of my body flat on the roof and was still able to chat to Mike who was standing next to me with the top half of his body out of the bus.

Close to the airport we went through a small town and I suddenly noticed how close the underside of a bridge was as we passed beneath it. I kept my head down until we were out of danger. I turned to say as much to Mike, but he was no longer standing next to me. To my horror, he was lying on the floor in a pool of blood. Sam was trying to stem the flow from Mike's head. We shouted at the bus driver to drive flat out to the Frommer, which he did. I rushed into reception to summon an ambulance which arrived promptly to take Mike to the nearest hospital.

The Dutch police arrived later that evening and took Sam and me away for questioning. They believed a fight must have occurred resulting in Mike's injuries. They took us to separate rooms and questioned us extensively. They eventually returned and let us go, having inspected the bridge and determined that Mike's head had indeed collided with the span. They struggled to believe anyone would be so stupid as to stick their head out of a moving bus, but as we both explained—separately—it was natural for us coming from Africa to travel on the backs of open vehicles, all having been brought up in the country.

The collision with the bridge stove in part of Mike's skull and once in hospital he spent a considerable time in intensive care, but never recovered sufficiently to be able to resume a career in aviation.

Sam and I were deeply concerned for his survival. We lost touch over time but I believe he moved to South Africa, married, and had children.

In retrospect it was a careless act that miserably terminated Mike's flying career. It was one of, if not the worst nights of my life, underlining the pain, suffering, and losses associated with every side of war.

By the middle of October all that remained prior to us being signed out as qualified on this aircraft type was the practical flying training and subsequent flight test. On October 15 the five remaining pilots boarded a DC-8 piloted by Adrian de Ras and flew to Shannon airport in Ireland. That afternoon we flew our first training sortie together and to be flying a large jet aircraft for the first time was truly awe-inspiring. Each pairing had its own instructor and by the end of the day each pilot had completed his first training detail. The following two days we completed further training routines, each with a final check ride on October 18. In the evenings the KLM instructors arranged exotic local experiences for us, and we spent a couple of evenings in Durty Nelly's, a famous pub in the village of Bunratty not far from Shannon airport, together with a memorable mediaeval banquet in Bunratty Castle.

We were now qualified on type and in those days that was considered good enough to start a career as an operational first officer. Today would-be pilots have to complete many sectors of line training and a line check before becoming fully operational. On my first flight I accompanied Captain 'Horse' Sweeny, a former South African Air Force World War Two Spitfire pilot and a veteran of the Korean War as well, from Libreville to Johannesburg on one of the sectors of our flight home.

For the rest of the year, I did not fly with 3 Squadron because I was too busy gaining valuable experience on the DC-8. Most of the captains with whom I flew were former RAF World War Two veterans or ex-Korean War pilots. It was a pleasure to share a cockpit with great characters such as Gus Tattersall, Horse Sweeny, and George Dyer. Additionally, we had an ex-French Air Force captain, Charles Goosens, as well as a former German Air Force pilot, Heinz Clapier.

Despite the British putting pressure on the various countries into which we operated, I managed to fly into the following airports by the end of the year: Amsterdam, Brussels, Palma de Majorca, Abidjan

(Ivory Coast), Lagos, Djibouti (Djibouti), Kigali (Rwanda), Nairobi, Paris Orly, Johannesburg, Kano (Nigeria), and of course our home base, Salisbury.

Pictured clockwise: 1) Early days on 3 Squadron, 1975. The aircrew wore camouflage, but the Dak didn't…yet. **2)** The tireless workhorses of the war. A DC-3 and an Alouette cross paths (top). **3)** A Dak in its new camouflage livery circa 1976. **4)** Another resupply mission for the SAS, mid 1970s.

Pictured clockwise: 1) RLI paratroops training on static lines, 1976. 2) A close shave. Inspecting the damage after clipping a tree at the Mabalauta SAS base in south-eastern Rhodesia, December 1977. 3) Top: The low-down, 1977. 3 Squadron Dakotas fly low into battle. Ground-hugging sorties lessened our exposure to enemy fire. 4) The shadow of the Dak on the ground shows how so much of our flying was performed just above tree height.

Pictured clockwise: 1) Adopt-a-dog. Me with Doris, Mike Borlace's, much-loved English sheep dog in the late 1970s. My family took care of him while Borlace languished in a Lusaka jail, accused of being a Rhodesian spy. **2)** Head in the clouds . . . feet in the dust. **3)** Me (top) and 3 Squadron Volunteer Reserve colleagues on our bush survival course at the Selous Scouts' Wafa Wafa training camp in the Zambezi Valley, 1979. **4)** Receiving the Military Forces Commendation (Operational) Medal from Air Vice Marshal Chris Damms, 1979.

Pictured clockwise: 1) The DC-7, on loan to the air force, in its new camouflage, 1979. 2) Local ingenuity. A converted landmine and ambush protected vehicle. In the foreground is Doris, Mike Borlace's English sheepdog, with my sons Sam and Nicholas in 1980. 3) Last days in the Rhodesian Air Force. David Barbour, me, and John Reid-Rowland in front of the 3 Squadron hangars, 1981. 4) Best of mates. Jeremy Lynch and me at 3 Squadron HQ New Sarum, Salisbury, 1980. 5) Death and honour … the Peterhouse war dead, and my Military Forces Commendation Medal in a publication celebrating Peterhouse School's quarter century, 1980.

Pictured clockwise: 1) End of a proud era. C Squadron SAS prepares to embark on its final ceremonial jump prior to disbanding, December 1980. **2)** Final curtain. The entire SAS Regiment on its symbolic final parachute jump, December 11 1980, prior to disbanding.

CHAPTER 12

Twin battles in the air—at home and abroad—1976

T he start of the year found me operating in Europe before flying home in early January, returning to 3 Squadron, and requalifying on the C-47. From now until the end of my career in the RhAF I flew for both outfits, alternating between flying the DC-8 and the DC-3.

On January 13 I had the honour and privilege to operate as first officer for Captain Jack Malloch on a round trip from Salisbury to Libreville and back. Henry Kinnear was the flight engineer. He and Malloch had operated together since the DC-4 days in the Congo. Captain Jack preferred an economy of conversation and said little in non-operational chat on both out and return sectors. Jean-Louis Domange met us on landing in Libreville, whisking the boss away in a black limousine. I subsequently learned that Malloch would use these trips to meet with his old colleague, the president of Gabon, Omar Bongo. After a couple of hours on the ground while the aircraft was unloaded and refuelled, Malloch re-appeared and without a word we departed for Salisbury.

Malloch had an obsession about wasting fuel by spooling up the engines unnecessarily prior to the final approach. The plan was always to delay the descent as long as possible so that the engines could be at idle until the last moment when applying power prior to landing. The basic equation was this: allow three miles for every 1,000 feet of descent, notably the three-degree profile. If you were flying at an altitude of 41,000 feet with a landing altitude of 5,000 feet you would expect to start your descent at 120 nautical miles from base (41,000 − 5,000 = 36,000/3 per 1,000 = 120).

Malloch would scorn such a conservative approach in an empty aircraft. To make Jack happy we would delay our descent to 80 miles from touchdown. We would then manage the profile to ensure we only applied thrust once the gear and flaps were fully extended on the final approach because we always carried out the descent with the engines at idle thrust and the throttles closed. A terse 'Well flown, laddie' from Malloch was considered high praise.

My first flight with Captain Jack was enjoyable and would not be our last though I was not to know it at the time. We flew together several times in the future, beginning just a week later with another Salisbury to Libreville turnaround, where he again disappeared with Domange for a few hours once we had landed in Libreville.

Towards the end of the month, I flew with George Dyer up to Paris Charles De Gaulle airport via Amsterdam for a night stop in Paris before operating a charter flight for Air France the next day from Paris to Caracas in Venezuela via the island of Santa Maria. It was my first Atlantic crossing. Since it was an Air France charter, our catering originated in Paris. We were amused and delighted to see that it came with a small bottle of red wine for each of us to accompany our main meal. Under the circumstances, who were we to question the habits and customs of the French; we were glad to toast our hosts halfway across the Atlantic.

3 Squadron demanded much of my flying time in February, March, and April. On a flight with Mike Russell, orders directed us to fly south-east along the border from Umtali (Mutare) over Malvernia in

Mozambique, on the border with Rhodesia, then on to Chiredzi. We had powerful cameras on board which were used to photograph the location of possible terrorist camps. Our intrusion attracted a barrage of small arms, rocket propelled grenades (RPGs) and 17mm anti-aircraft fire, but with no damage to our aircraft.

Additionally, with Affretair, which changed its name from Air Trans Africa in 1975, I was able to increase my list of airports into which I flew, among them Tehran, Kuwait, Comoros, Seychelles, and Reims in France to collect aircraft parts and armaments for the RhAF. Bombay (now Mumbai), left me with the wrong kind of memories where, on a night stop, I picked up a severe case of Delhi belly after eating a curry. I had the runs for several days which made flying most uncomfortable, especially on the long flight we undertook directly from Paris Orly back to Salisbury.

In the meantime, in the background the British were putting enormous pressure on various countries to deny us overflight clearance. At home, while the bush war was generally well-contained throughout the country, there were still many problems on many fronts that needed attention. Early in May, our freight operations froze for a few days with no flying at all on the DC-7 or the two DC-8s. None of us was sure when or even whether we would start flying again, or be paid. By then, Affretair and not Air Gabon Cargo employed us and the identifying livery carried the airline's name on the side of the aircraft. After a few days of high level secrecy, all seemed to be well and we resumed operations, never being made any the wiser.

By mid-May I had completed the necessary checks and requirements for the issue of my air force wings as well as qualifying as a C category or junior captain permitted to fly in command on routine operations. (Until then my great air force mate, Jerry Lynch, referred to me as the wingless wonder.) The air force conducted my wings award ceremony in the ante room of the officer's mess at New Sarum air base. My wife and mother attended, and I was additionally humbled and pleased with the presence of Captain Jack at the invitation of the issuing officer, Air Marshal Chris Damms and my Squadron CO, George Alexander. It was rewarding to see my family chatting amiably to both my seniors over champagne after the ceremony.

The RhAF squadrons had callsigns assigned to the various pilots. Our CO, George Alexander, was Alpha 3, B Flight Commander, Ivan Holshausen, was Bravo 3, C Flight Commander, Bob D'Hotman, was Charlie 3, and so on through the squadron for the rest of the captains.

VR captains started from the bottom of the alphabet and as I was now the fourth qualified VR captain, I received the callsign Whiskey 3. Before I could work as a captain on operations I had to complete a bush tour under supervision because a Dakota was now deployed at each FAF to be used as required on local operations. I was delighted to be deployed with my close friend, Jerry Lynch. We spent a week at Rutenga in the central south west of the country, but for three days did no flying as there was no requirement for us to get airborne. Over the other days we were kept busy flying to airfields in the south of the country, delivering personnel and provisions.

Jerry had trained in the Royal Navy and loved low flying which he demonstrated on many occasions, teaching me the fundamentals of low altitude work over both land and water. We once flew across Lake Kariba, where he dropped close enough to the surface to pick up spray from the propellers skimming the water, unnerving me in the process. While we were on the bush tour, we would regularly fly into Boli, a stunted dirt strip in the south of the country. The dynamics of landing on such a short runway stirred up storm clouds of dust which would settle on the aircraft. Jerry took regular offence, believing it made the aircraft look older and more decrepit than necessary. We were based at Rutenga and on the way back we would fly over the sugar cane fields south of Chiredzi. His remedy for the squalor was to fly through the towering sprays of the circular irrigation rigs watering crops grown over a vast acreage in the Lowveld. This constituted in his mind the aircraft having its regular shower.

The week after my first bush tour, I re-joined Affretair, flying with

George Dyer to Tehran via the Comoros and Seychelles. We were meant to spend two days only in Tehran, but something went awry with the next charter. We had to endure nine days on three days' allowances. Even though the country was still under the rule of the Shah, and life was relatively normal compared to the years following the revolution, the lack of funds made the trip tedious. We eventually made it home via Bombay and Paris.

On June 15, while on callup duty with 3 Squadron, I was detailed to fly my first sortie as a captain. As a co-pilot you would perform all the supportive duties before the flight, paying scant attention to the captain and his responsibilities. This time, it was me briefing the troops and the crew, including a para dispatcher. I felt both self-conscious and newly aware of the burden of responsibility now on my shoulders.

For the next few months, I was busy flying both with the air force and Affretair, logging about 80 hours a month, a substantial workload in those days when civilian aviation limited us to a monthly 60. In July I served my second bush tour based at Buffalo Range/Chiredzi as co-pilot to Vic Cook. There, I experienced my first fireforce callout.

The Rhodesian security forces developed the concept of fireforce as a flexible and effective frontline counter-terrorist response. Typically, it consisted of three types of aircraft and assault troops based at a FAF. They would respond quickly when troops on the ground detected or engaged terrorists they may have been watching and monitoring for days. Once the fireforce callout was initiated all the aircraft involved would get airborne.

A senior air force pilot would coordinate the air movements from an Alouette III helicopter K-car (K standing for kill or command). The K-car was equipped with a MG 20mm canon firing high explosive incendiary (HEI) shells. The K-car crew was made up of the air force pilot, army commander, and a technician/gunner. Once close to the target area, the K-car would maintain radio contact with the observation post (OP) or the ground troop commander. They would either describe the location of the terrorists or, if close enough, throw a smoke grenade into their midst, giving a direction finder to the K-car. The K-car would adopt an anticlockwise orbit of the target area, to accommodate the cannon fixed in the chopper's port or left door. It would orbit at between 750 and 1,000 feet, enabling a clear view of the target area and providing an ideal height for maximum effectiveness of the 20mm weapon. The altitude also provided a level of protection from the often erratic small arms fire.

Invariably the K-car would open fire immediately on sighting the terrorists, the results of which would then determine the course of the ensuing action. If any of the group survived or fled, the commander had at his disposal three G-cars (G standing for gunships). These were also Alouette III helicopters armed with twin .303 Browning machine guns. Each G-car crew had the pilot and his technician/gunner and carried a stick or squad of four fully armed troops. The army commander would then instruct each G-car as to where to drop his troops in order to create a stop line or to assist in engaging the enemy if a firefight had broken out. Also at the K-car commander's disposal was a ground attack fixed wing aircraft, the Reims-Cessna 337 Lynx, which had replaced the earlier Percival Provost. The Lynx's were armed with twin Browning .303 machine guns mounted above the wing and 37mm SNEB rockets, locally made mini Alpha bombs (cluster bombs), mini Golf bombs (200kg blast and shrapnel bomb), and frantans (frangible napalm drop tanks).

Depending on the location and surrounding terrain, the use of the Lynx was a valuable tool in the deployment of the various weapons at his disposal. The SNEB rocket was effective against terrorists hiding among the many rocky outcrops that characterised the country. Napalm was also useful where terrorists had hidden in caves.

Should the group have split up into smaller groups or individuals, or bomb-shelled as fireforce troops termed the tactic, the commanders would fall back on the Dakota. It held up to five sticks of four paratroopers per stick and was the last of the aircraft in the fireforce reaction group. Generally a G-car pilot would find a suitable landing area for the paratroops and deploy a smoke grenade to help the Dakota pilot calculate the wind drift before despatching his troops. The usual drop height above the ground for deploying troops was about 800 feet.

Security force guidelines recommended 400 feet as the minimum drop height for paratroops. However, in practice it became 300 feet. The absolute minimum without endangering life was 250 feet but the lowest recorded exit height was by a Rhodesia Light Infantry (RLI) troopie at a bone-rattling 217 feet.

RLI troops made more operational jumps than any other military unit in history. The record held by an individual belongs to an RLI corporal, Des Archer, with 73 jumps between 1977 and the end of the war. Allied paratroops in the World War Two were considered veterans after just one operational jump. Our troops regularly made two operational jumps a day.

Over the previous few months I had been extremely busy flying, had hardly any time with my family, and taken no leave for well over a year, so I was granted a month off. In July we flew to the UK via Johannesburg and spent a pleasant few weeks enjoying the hottest summer England had ever experienced. It was a palpable relief to escape the war and the tension of our illegal globe-trotting.

By now Affretair had a contract to undertake 50 flights into Tehran delivering cages housing about five thousand day old chicks per trip. We used to fly from Salisbury to the Seychelles where we would refuel before continuing on to Tehran, off-loading, and flying on to Amsterdam, all in one trip involving 15 hours of actual flying, impossible under any other circumstances. Curiously, most of the time the chicks, would chirp noisily in unison, when, for no discernible reason, they would all stop at exactly the same moment, as though under the baton of a stern conductor. Absolute silence would reign for a short while and suddenly they would all start up again, precisely on cue. I never fathomed the answer.

In October, I did my third bush tour, my first as commander. My co-pilot was a Rhodesian friend, Richard Calder, who had been at Cranwell before me. He had qualified and then stayed on in the RAF for a few years before returning to Rhodesia as a chartered accountant. He was now a member of the VR on callup duty. We were based at Chiredzi for nine days and were fully occupied throughout, flying shuttle and resupply duties.

Flying, as I knew from my experience as an accident investigator, has hazardous and sometimes fatal moments. During the callup we had to take off from Zaka, a remote strip south-east of Fort Victoria (now Masvingo). We momentarily experienced an almost total loss of power in both engines and only just managed to recover maximum power before we would have hit the trees at the end of the runway.

The technician who was based with us and took care of the aircraft was on board the flight. He confessed once we had landed that he had forgotten to check the oil levels during his daily service before we left. Like almost any mechanical device, oil is vital, in our case for both the engine and the propeller systems. On the second take off of the day we had insufficient oil to supply both at the same time. The oil level was well below the minimum required for dispatch when he checked back at base. He was blushingly contrite and apologetic. I left it at that. These near-crises happen in the stress of war and in the operational theatre.

On the same tour we regularly flew re-supply missions into and out of Boli, not far from the Mozambican border in the southern part of the country and bordering the South Gonarezhou National Park. Taking off on one flight, I found it extremely difficult to raise the tail. It was too late to abort the take off because the strip was shorter than most. I had the yoke (control column or stick) hard against the instrument panel in a desperate attempt to get the aircraft into flying attitude. We just staggered over the trees and finally, as our speed increased, I was able to relieve the forward pressure on the stick, but had almost full nose-down trim as well. We managed to land at Chiredzi, forced to keep a higher than normal approach speed because when the speed dropped too far I ran out of elevator control, with the stick almost fully forward.

On investigation, we discovered that a number of crates had been loaded too far towards the rear of the aircraft. Worse, the weight of the cargo was marked in kilos instead of pounds without anyone noticing. A quick calculation established that we had taken off nearly three tons, or 30 per cent overweight. It was a close escape and another lesson learned in the urgent turbulence of war in the bush.

Another adventure saw us arrive back at Chiredzi late in the afternoon, hoping we had finished after a long day and looking forward to a cold *chibuli*, or beer. A relayed message tasked us with a casevac (casualty evacuation) mission to rescue a seriously wounded soldier who was being transported to Zaka, a small, isolated, and hardly-used strip in the middle of the country.

Originally the task was assigned to the 4 Squadron Lynx pilot, Mick Delport, but he pointed out that with thunderstorms in the area, and since he was a single pilot operation, it would be safer to call on our multi crew Dakota instead. We agreed and side-lining our thirsts, took off for Zaka. The horizon soon disappeared in the ominous clouds of the storm ahead, made worse by nightfall.

Zaka is surrounded by hills. Even in daylight, it was not a pleasant airfield into which to fly. For once, the thunderstorm played to our advantage; we picked up the outline of the hills in the lightning flashes as we descended into a pitch-black, moonless night.

The ground troops understood the danger, and set out a series of goose-neck flares. However, heavy rain left only a few sparsely spaced lights, making it difficult to discern the parameters and dimensions of the airstrip as a whole, let alone the restricted landing area. Arriving overhead, I was just able to make out that this was the strip below me. The troops had also cleverly positioned a vehicle at the beginning of the strip with its headlights shining along the runway. We managed to land successfully and uplifted the wounded Rhodesian African Rifles (RAR) soldier to Salisbury where he was operated on and made a full recovery. When we landed, my clothes were sweat-soaked from the tension of two of the riskiest night landings and take-offs in my career, knowing that more than one life was at stake that night in Zaka. Soon after, I received a letter of gratitude from the wounded man's commanding officer thanking me for my role in saving his life.

On reflection, I still feel a vestigial sense of injustice at the memory of those who accused us of fighting a purely racial war. The historical, social, economic, and political forces at work then—and even now—were more complex and difficult than such a simplistic notion could possibly explain. The numbers alone tell a radically different story: the Rhodesian forces as a whole contained as many black soldiers, if not more, than white. Stories abound of black brothers fighting on either side of the conflict, torn by beliefs for which they were prepared to sacrifice their lives. For me the complexion of the soldiers we dropped out of the aircraft or flew to rescue when wounded was irrelevant. The defence of freedom against a declared Marxist tyranny that would come to its brutal fruition was worthy of the struggle.

In early December I embarked on a long trip with Roger Brackley, flying through the Seychelles to night-stop in Muscat, and then on to Tehran before flying to Amsterdam. From there a couple of days later we journeyed to Lagos and back. Lagos was our least favoured destination; we had to wait most of the day on the aircraft while it was unloaded before winging back either to Amsterdam or Palma de Majorca. Happiness to us all was V1 (committed to take off speed) out of Lagos.

Once back in Amsterdam we were briefed that on our next flight we would be carrying VIP passengers who were bringing with them an item of supreme sensitivity. On December 11 we set off from Amsterdam to Palma de Majorca where we would refuel before continuing on to Libreville and subsequently home. Our two mysterious VIP guests, whom we did not meet initially, were already installed with their precious cargo in the back of the aeroplane where two seats were also fixed for passenger use.

On the take-off roll, just as we got airborne, we winced at a resounding bang accompanied by a significant thump underneath the aircraft close to the undercarriage. After retracting the gear, a red warning light activated indicating we had a problem. The prescribed procedure called for us to reduce speed and lower the undercarriage again, which we did successfully, but safety and mechanical codes required us to return to land at Majorca. We had a further issue: we were over the allowable landing weight, so we had to spend a minimum of 30 minutes out to sea dumping sufficient fuel to lower our weight to the permitted limit. We landed without incident to discover the problem arose from a wheel rim detaching at high speed and smashing into the adjacent engine cowl, causing substantial damage. Replacing the wheel and checking the engine would take some time so the decision was made to stop overnight. We were now given the all-clear to meet our passengers who, while isolated in the cargo deck, had had no way of communicating with us or us with them. We were pleasantly surprised to meet two men of a similar age to us. They admitted they had felt concern at the thump on take-off but assumed, since we kept flying, that we had the situation under control. Luckily, both had British passports, so clearing Spanish immigration was not a problem, but we had to ensure that the aircraft, and more particularly their precious payload, would be safely guarded. We arranged the appropriate security and retired to a hotel for the night while repairs took place, still none the wiser as to the identity of our passengers nor the contents of their consignment.

By the next morning the aircraft was again serviceable, and we resumed our journey southwards to Salisbury via Libreville and Johannesburg. Our other DC-8, TR-LQR, was waiting for us at Libreville, which then took our two passengers and their top secret freight directly to Salisbury. Their identity and the nature of their shipment is a story for a later chapter.

Under sanctions, which destroyed many businesses and livelihoods, both black and white, people tried to find ways to protect or move their money out of the country. Of course some sought to smuggle out their wealth or enrich themselves. Most abided by the country's internal currency regulations. Others willingly cooperated with our sanctions-busting activities or invented schemes of their own to export commodities and earn desperately-needed foreign exchange on which the nation's survival depended.

For example, a farmer who ran a successful cattle breeding ranch had managed to secure a deal whereby he would transport a breeding herd of young cows to Brazil. In time he would follow and set up a similar trade there. The necessary clearances took some time to obtain but on New Year's Eve we left from Salisbury with a load of about 50 prime heifers. We flew initially to Libreville to refuel before setting off across the Atlantic to land in San Salvador in Brazil about eight hours later.

We had no official reception party and none of us could fathom the sense of flying into a foreign, third world country, especially in South America, on New Year's Day, carrying live animals. Livestock on international exchanges always need a vet to certify them on landing, as well as a plethora of other documentation. The intended destination for the cattle was indeed Brazil, but because of the subterfuge of the operation and the associated complications involved in the paperwork we were told we had to leave Brazil immediately or have the aircraft impounded. Confusion reigned.

We contacted base and we were told that we could fly to Paraguay where a third party would accept the cattle. The air in the cargo hold was rank with the overpowering odour of bovine urine and dung. The animals were stressed and in dire need of water, which we could not deliver on board. We made for Asuncion in Paraguay, which was not a long flight. In hindsight, had we known what was about to take place we could have kept an engine running to provide ventilation for the poor creatures suffering in the hold of the aircraft. The aircraft needed a ground power unit to start the engines, but none was available when we arrived, nor for most of the next nine hours we sat on the ground waiting to offload. The load master did what he could by opening the cargo and back doors to the aircraft in an attempt to circulate some air through the cargo compartment. We could only wait helplessly and in mounting distress until belatedly some Paraguayan officials arrived. A high loader was produced and proceeded to unload the pallets containing the cattle.

To our horror, every last creature was dead. Asphyxiation and dehydration had killed them all. It was an unholy bungle, and the sight of these beautiful, young creatures dead on top of each other filled us with a grief I hope I never experience again. As crew, we were denied further entry into the country and as soon as we had unloaded our tortured cargo of death, we departed for Sao Paulo in Brazil, our original destination. I could not help but reflect that under normal circumstances we would have flown there direct, cleared customs without incident, and delivered our innocent payload alive. Sleepless for more than 40 hours on a cruelly futile mission, we slept the night and made the gruelling flight directly to Salisbury. It was an appalling start to 1977.

Over the year I added a long list of new airports I had flown to with Affretair: Santa Maria in the Azores, Caracas in Venezuela, Kuwait, Rheims, Seychelles, Tehran, Lubumbashi in the Democratic Republic of the Congo, Comoros, Muscat, Baghdad, Dubai, Franceville (Gabon), Salvador, Asuncion, Sao Paulo, and Lisbon. This exotic menu of foreign ports demonstrates how successful the airline was at the time despite the attempts of the British to shut us down.

CHAPTER THIRTEEN

The strain mounts, the war escalates—1977

T he general situation in Rhodesia was no longer in our favour. Militarily we still held our own internally, but terrorist numbers were increasing by the day with more of the black population, particularly its youth, volunteering to fight for the cause, or facing violent coercion. Once trained, they were transferred into staging camps outside the country before moving back across the border. Once inside the country they would splinter and present more difficult targets.

Through strategic necessity, the emphasis shifted towards hitting the enemy outside the country while still grouped in large numbers. Politically, the situation had deteriorated. In September 1976, the American Secretary of State, Henry Kissinger, visited South Africa and summoned Rhodesian Prime Minister, Ian Smith, to a meeting with South African President, John Vorster. With a five point plan drawn up by the British, Ian Smith was forced to accept majority rule within two years. In turn the terrorist leaders agreed to halt all guerrilla activities but failed to uphold their end of the bargain, so the war continued unabated. However, Smith began working towards creating a multi-racial government led by Bishop Abel Muzorewa, a black moderate thought acceptable to the majority of the population.

The pressure applied by the British Government on various countries to our north also began to impact on Affretair's operations. Zambia and Angola temporarily withdrew permission to all Gabonese-registered aircraft overflying their countries, resulting in much longer flight times to Libreville and beyond. We now had to fly west in parallel with the Angolan border before crossing the coast, turning north, and flying over the ocean to our destination.

In his past, Jack Malloch had been involved in assisting the Omanis, particularly during the peaceful coup staged by Qaboos bin Said, who deposed his father, Said bin Taimur, as head of state. He now used his influence to establish an Omani freight airline recently registered in the name of Cargoman with one DC-8. Affretair had two DC-8s, TR-LVK and TR-LQR. At the beginning of January I flew QR but by the end of the month I flew the same aircraft, re registered as A4O-PA which now belonged to Cargoman. In the process we pilots now held three professional licenses: Rhodesian, Gabonese, and Omani. I still have my official Omani examiner certificate for the time I became a training captain with the airline. We were meant to remain separate from the crew flying the Gabonese aircraft, and vice versa, but it never worked because we were still effectively flying for the same airline—Affretair.

In mid-January, I started my fourth bush tour, this time with one of my Affretair colleagues and close friend, Richard Hayes. Unfortunately, the crew we were replacing at Chiredzi, Dave Mallett (ex RAF) and Peter Barnett, our close colleague with whom Richard and I had trained on the DC-8 course, were killed the day before when their aircraft collided with power lines crossing a riverbed along which they were flying.

The first day Richard and I were together we flew a long high altitude low opening (HALO) paratroop mission for the SAS, deep into Mozambique. We would fly in at a height of between 13,000 and

18,000 feet. Approaching the target we would alert the dispatchers with a 'red light on' signal, advising them to prepare the paratroops for the jump. Often the despatch of containerised weapons and supplies preceded jumps. At the command 'green light on' out the container would go, followed swiftly by the troops who would free fall focusing on the box whose parachute was triggered at low level by a barometric opening device. They would then deploy their own chutes and follow the box to the ground. If no extra supplies were needed for the operation, they simply free fell in formation before opening their chutes at a minimum safe height. The HALO method of deploying troops into enemy territory became commonplace. At those altitudes, noise from the aircraft was minimal and since we kept the aircraft on its original course for some time it was difficult for anyone on the ground to know if or when troops were deployed, even if they suspected this was the case.

Whenever deaths occurred on the squadron, only pilots who were not in the bush or otherwise engaged on active service would attend the funerals. It saddened Richard and me to miss farewelling our good friend, Peter.

We spent a week at Buffalo Range/Chiredzi busily flying during the day and undertaking several cross border resupply missions to the SAS at night. The resupply missions, particularly those flown at night, were always stressful and energy sapping.

Unlike modern aircraft which use a radio altimeter to give pilots an exact altitude, our aircraft carried barometric instruments that displayed differing air pressures as a measure of height. They were never as accurate and could often fluctuate from a radio altimeter's readings by as much as 50 feet. We would set the altimeter to the barometric pressure (QNH) at our departure airfield which, if correct, would then display the altitude of the airfield above sea level. Barometric pressure can vary significantly over relatively short distances and with one millibar of pressure equating to more than 30 feet we could fly into an area where the pressure had changed by a couple of millibars. That meant we could, in reality, be flying at a height of 60 feet higher or lower than indicated on the altimeter.

Another problem with flying at night over the area known as the Lowveld, was a metrological phenomenon called *guti*, or dense, low cloud. It was usually only about 200 feet thick. but the base would normally sit at between 100 and 200 feet above the ground with good visibility below. Often the SAS unit we were resupplying would be a considerable distance away from our departure point, deep in enemy territory across the border. On such nights we had to decide whether to fly underneath, making it difficult to navigate because at that height it was impossible to pinpoint your position easily. We faced the additional hazard of attracting the enemy's attention should we fly over them. Or should we climb through the cloud and set course for our rendezvous flying at a safe height over this thick blanket?

Resupply missions for the troops on the ground were essential. It was also vital that we found them on our first run because if we overflew them and had to circle back we would immediately compromise their position. We had to navigate precisely and accurately. Of course our aircraft were not fitted with GPS or any such sophisticated equipment of the modern era.

Before we departed we would draw a line on a map (even they were rudimentary), measure the bearing to fly, measure the distance, lay off the drift due to the wind and rely on our basic navigation which was heading and time (time equalling distance). If we had flown the sector below the cloud, we would hope we had got it right, that the ground troops would hear us, and instruct us to switch our navigation lights on so that they could direct us during the final stages. We were fortunate in that the terrain was slightly lower than the area we had left, meaning we would still be below the cloud at about 250 feet above ground (or so we thought from reading the altimeter). This was the optimum height for dropping the boxes whose parachutes were attached to a static lines which would automatically deploy the chutes on exiting the aircraft.

Since we could not see the exact location of the troops, they had been trained to control the drop from the ground. Once they heard us and subsequently sighted the aircraft's navigation lights, they would direct us to turn right or left until we were heading directly for their position. The command 'red light on' would alert the dispatchers in the back to get the boxes into position and at the command 'green light on' they would despatch the boxes. We would maintain the same heading for quite some time to avoid compromise.

The real problem arose if we had decided to fly the route above the cloud. At the appropriate time to descend we would push the nose of the aircraft down and fly into the all-enveloping cloud, watching and waiting for the colour of our surrounds to darken further, hopefully before the altitude on our altimeter indicated we were at zero feet or actually lower. It was terrifying, but in time we became accustomed to it. We learned that if you flew in cloud at night near the ground the colour of the light was soft and opaque. As soon as you broke cloud the surrounding atmosphere became much darker, almost black.

On occasions, if I was uncertain of my height, I would switch on the landing lights momentarily and dive towards the ground. Once I could see green vegetation in the lights, we could then cross check the altimeter and establish our height above the ground reasonably accurately. I freely confess I found sorties under these conditions mentally and physically draining. Joy for us on resupply nights was a clear sky with a full moon. But we were also painfully aware that clear conditions were less favourable for the ground troops who faced an increased risk of having their positions betrayed. The voice over the radio saying 'Thanks guys, good drop' was the sweetest message we could receive.

Fear is the single greatest emotion in any war; fear of death, of serious or permanent injury, and even of failure. In the context of our operations, any modern pilot reading the description above of our resupply missions would understand the fear involved. Yes, it was frightening but I can honestly say of all the re-supply sorties I flew for the SAS, all were successful bar one which, though not my fault and without harmful results, still blemishes my sense of a perfect record. More of that later. It was our greatest reward because we knew those supplies were desperately needed by brave men fighting for their lives and ours far from home in hostile territory. I would arrive back at base soaked through but at the same time exhilarated.

Coming under enemy fire with the distinct possibility of being wounded or killed is an almost sickeningly sobering experience. I would like to meet the aviator or soldier who maintains they never experienced fear prior to, or during combat. Again, I can only speak for myself but yes, I wondered and worried as to how I would react when hostile fire came my way.

I can declare my overriding stress stemmed from my fear that I would let myself down in front of my colleagues by displaying a lack of moral fibre. Early in my time in command, I was on a resupply mission for the SAS, carried out unusually in the late afternoon because of a critical need for the materiel. As the SAS controller on the ground directed us into the final stages of the drop, I could hear and see flashes and bangs all around the aircraft as we came under heavy small arms and rocket propelled grenade (RPG) fire. The controller, who could see what was happening, confirmed over the radio what we already knew. We continued with the drop, which was successful, and the firing ceased. My permanent memory is one of almost overwhelming relief. I had faced my baptism of fire, continued with the mission according to plan, and had not let my colleagues down. I had made it. I now knew I could contain my fear, keeping that nauseating feeling of cowardice at bay and coping with the task in hand.

While the war continued to accelerate internally, much of the emphasis of Selous Scouts and SAS operations shifted to hitting the enemy in training or transit camps across the border in Mozambique. Special Branch police had received radio intercepts that a large group of terrorists would occupy a substantial transit camp adjacent to

Madulo Pan, some 50 miles south of the Rhodesian border and well over 60 miles south of Chiredzi between January 10 and 12.

The Rhodesian military high command, known as Combined Operations Headquarters (ComOps), decided that an attack on the camp would take place on the morning of January 12. On the afternoon of January 10 we flew south across the border, climbing to 14,000 feet. Close to the pan we advised the dispatchers, and soon Captain Chris 'Schulie' Schulenburg and his reconnaissance teammate, Sergeant Steven Mpofu, free-fell from the aircraft. Those knowledgeable in the field consider these two the best reconnaissance team in the world, ever. Both were soon to be decorated, Schulenburg with the Grand Cross of Valour (GCV, Rhodesian equivalent of the Victoria Cross, of which only two were ever awarded), and Mpofu the Silver Cross of Rhodesia (SCR, equivalent to the Distinguished Service Order, and one rank below the GCV). They would, over the next day, confirm the camp was indeed fully occupied and at the same time set up electronic flares which would guide the Rhodesian bombers to their target.

At 0400 on the morning of January 12, three Canberra bombers electronically activated the flares that had been planted to guide them, and bombed the camp. The concept was that at that time of the morning the enemy would be awake and out in the open. The alpha bombs would bounce and explode above the ground causing carnage. At first light chopper-borne troops would deploy to mop up and secure the camp.

Pre-dawn, an armada of aircraft set off from Chiredzi. Observing the strung-out line of pulsing rotator beacons as each helicopter joined the formation was unforgettable. The beacon lights were switched off once the light improved and the choppers regained full visibility. We followed up in the Dak with sticks of RLI paratroops and drums of avgas on board to parachute in when the helicopters needed refuelling. We followed the strike force to the camp and were now orbiting some way off, but close enough to observe the sequence of events. Two

Hawker Hunter aircraft orbited ready to be called in for an airstrike and a Canberra with a full bomb load loitered at high altitude.

Unknown to the attacking force, the majority of the alpha bombs failed to bounce, instead penetrating a sandy base into clay where they exploded with minimal impact. FRELIMO, the socialist Mozambican forces, had been alerted and sent in a column to assist the terrorists. Consequently, when the K-cars arrived over the camp, they ran into considerable small arms and anti-aircraft fire. It was something to behold, watching the lines of tracers arcing into the sky like a firework display all but enveloping the helicopters.

Mike Borlace, legendary 7 Squadron fireforce chopper pilot, and one of just five holders of the Silver Cross of Rhodesia (SCR), was in the lead K-car. I still recall and admire his calm voice announcing that he was under savage fire and intended closing in to neutralise the responsible gun emplacement. He and his gunner eliminated the nest of 12.7mm heavy machine guns. Red section—the Hunters— were called in to deliver an airstrike on the camp which they did, but it was deemed more fire power was needed so they called up the orbiting fully-loaded Canberra and urged it into the attack. It never appeared. No-one knew at the time, but it broke cloud above heavily defended Malvernia, was hit by anti-aircraft fire and crashed, kill- ing all three people on board, pilot Ian Donaldson, navigator David Hawkes, and observer Selous Scout Captain Rob Warracker (SCR).

Major Bert Sachs, overseeing the operation from a fixed wing aircraft overhead, could see and hear what had happened and called off the operation. In time Rhodesia established that few terrorists had been killed, but many were wounded and lost limbs. They deemed it a psychological benefit since limbless combatants have a depressing effect on recruitment. We returned to base with our fuel drums and troops still on board. In my view, although we took some lessons from the operation, the attack on Madulo Pan was more disaster than success.

On the same tour a Dakota arrived carrying the two mystery passengers Roger Brackley and I had flown from Amsterdam through Majorca. Nigel 'Toobs' Charles, I was soon to learn, was the squadron commander of the Sultan of Oman's Air Force (SOAF) Hunter squadron. He and his colleague, Mike Sharp, were visiting all the forward airfields in Rhodesia demonstrating in practical terms the operation of the SAM 7 missile that the Omani forces had captured during their recent war with Yemen. The special cargo we brought home was the weapon itself, hence the secrecy.

Recent intelligence had indicated that the terrorist organisations had by now acquired several of these missiles and were infiltrating them into the country. The Strela-2 surface to air missile (or SAM-7) was a Russian-made, light weight, shoulder-fired missile system. It is designed to target aircraft at low altitudes, with an infrared homing guidance capability and a high explosive warhead. When they saw I was also part of the military establishment they were happy to acknowledge on the need-to know-basis and I was security cleared. None of us could foretell then the deadly harvest of innocent civilians these weapons would soon reap.

No sooner had Richard and I finished our bush tour than we flew to Amsterdam to undergo our DC-8 simulator checks in the KLM facility with our company training captain, Eddie Morrist.

Late in January I flew with our other training captain, 'Clem' Clements to Muscat via the Seychelles. By coincidence our two passengers were Toobs Charles and Mike Sharp returning to their Middle East base. I persuaded Clem to allow them a spell at the controls of the DC-8, with Mike at the column on our descent into Muscat. Knowing the ATC personnel, he requested and received permission for a typical Hunter arrival, thrilling us at low level over and at times through some of the wide canyons south of Muscat airport.

That night in the bar of the Gulf Hotel, we cemented a firm and continuing friendship that saw them both bring their girlfriends to stay on a visit back to Rhodesia the following year. Such was our mutual trust and respect, on one of my later trips to Muscat they flew me down to their base at Thumrait (Midway) and organised me a couple of trips in their twin seat Hawker Hunter. Whenever in the future we flew into Salalah or Muscat, we would call them up in advance and revel in an escort of up to four Hunters at a time formatting on our wingtips.

The following day Clem Clements, Harry Smith, our flight engineer, and I positioned to Bahrain, and on January 31 we flew from there to Singapore. Singapore Airlines had contracted this new freight company, Cargoman, to carry out a long freight charter flight for them. We returned the next day flying back to Bahrain via Colombo.

While the aircraft, Papa Alpha, was parked on the apron, I noticed a fellow in civilian clothes wandering around under the aircraft, apparently inspecting it. When I asked if I could help, he replied in a very British accent that he was a keen plane spotter and had secured permission to examine this unusual aircraft. I was unconvinced. When he noticed that the underside of the wing still had the recent markings of QR faintly visible, I deduced that he was from the British Consulate intent on a good snoop. I could do nothing except smile and bid him farewell before a week's flying to Paris Orly, Zurich, Bahrain, back to Orly, all on the same charter, and finally home in Victor Kilo via Libreville and Lubumbashi.

Over the next couple of weeks, I went through a series of standardisation upgrade checks with the 3 Squadron CO George Alexander since my command category was being upgraded from C to B. It meant I could take over some of the more important flights as the commander.

On March 1 I flew as co-pilot with the CO again, this time to Gwenora, the airstrip especially constructed on the prime minister, Ian Smith's farm, near Selukwe, now Shurugwi. Our passengers were the prime minister and his wife, Janet. Normally, only the captain would have the pleasure of meeting VIP passengers, but the premier made a point of visiting the cockpit to greet and thank us. Later in the month we returned to Gwenora to collect them both. They were a charming couple.

On March 4 I embarked on a long series of flights over two weeks with Roger Brackley, which took us to yet more new destinations: Amman in Jordan, Dubai, Sanaa in Yemen, and Jeddah in Saudi Arabia. During this trip we passed through Muscat on a couple of occasions, which gave us the opportunity to have a medical check for the continued validity of our Omani licenses. We met up with our pals Toobs, Sharpie, and some of their SOAF Hunter squadron colleagues in the bar of the Gulf Hotel, fortunately after the medical. The outcome might not have been quite as successful if our session had been the night before. Most of them, as ex-navy and air force pilots, drank copiously as a compensation for living in a desert environment.

On March 24 I flew with Captain Jack and our chief flight engineer, John Hodges, from Salisbury to Yamoussoukro, the new capital of the Ivory Coast in west Africa. As with other flights with the Boss, a car arrived when we landed to pick him up and after some time, he returned having paid a visit to President Felix Houphouet-Boigny, another African leader with whom Malloch had an excellent relationship.

In late April I was called up for my fifth bush tour, this time based at Fort Victoria (Masvingo). During our week there, not only did we undertake several cross border resupply missions but were also involved in five fireforce callouts which involved us dropping our troops directly into battle on two occasions, both of which were successful with all the terrorists accounted for.

On May 14 I left Salisbury with Gus Tattersall (a former World War Two pilot who was involved in the bloody September 1944 raid on Arnhem) on a two week trip that took us among other places to Cairo and Rotterdam. On May 24 we positioned to Ostend from where we were going to take the ferry to Dover the next day as we were due to carry out our first charter from the UK. We thought we would attract less attention if we went into the UK by the back door, so to speak. However, no sooner had we arrived in the UK, we were recalled. We retraced our steps and arrived back in Amsterdam that evening. By the next day the charter was back on. On this occasion, as time was short, we actually flew on KLM to Gatwick. We checked into the airport hotel, visited a local pub that evening and were ready the next morning for the arrival of Quebec Romeo.

Mid-morning, I received a phone call from Gus to say the charter had been cancelled and that the British were onto us; we should get out of the UK as quickly as possible. The agent who had set up the charter drove me to Heathrow from where I caught a flight to Amsterdam. We were the first and last Cargoman crew to travel to the UK while Rhodesia still existed.

On May 31, Jerry Lynch and his co-pilot on the day, Brucie Collocott, took off at night from Mapai, an airfield in Mozambique that our troops had earlier captured. As the aircraft began its climb it came under heavy fire from both small arms and RPG weapons which took out the starboard engine. Jerry managed to control the aircraft and put it back on the ground. Unfortunately, Brucie was killed instantly, and the aircraft totally destroyed by fire. It was a painful loss of a fine officer and a much-needed aircraft.

Every evening, a news bulletin on Rhodesian Television (RTV, a subsidiary of the Rhodesian Broadcasting Corporation) would commence with 'Rhodesian Security Forces regret to announce the death in action of …' We would hold our collective breath, hoping not to recognise any names, but on that night, there was no avoiding the sudden reality of his death. I felt as though someone had punched me in the stomach. Knowing he was crewed with Jerry, I feared the worst and phoned my friend immediately. He had just arrived home after his ordeal and relayed the sequence of events.

I was able to attend Brucie's funeral on June 6. The lone trumpeter playing the *Last Post* was a feature of all the military funerals we attended, and to this day I cannot hear those mournful notes without my thoughts drifting back to all those decent, brave, lovely men who lie buried under Zimbabwean soil. They also cause me to reflect the futility of those years. On deeper analysis, I would not have changed what we did, but perhaps those making the decisions at a political level should have thought more about the consequences.

The rest of June passed with my flying about 80 hours with both outfits collectively, adding Abu Dhabi to my list of airports into which I had flown.

Early in July I embarked on another two week pattern with Roger Brackley, under contract to Air France to fulfil a number of charters out of Paris Charles de Gaulle airport, which took us to Ndjamena in Chad, Douala in Cameroon, Ouagadougou in Burkina Faso (formerly the Republic of Upper Volta), Milan, and Kinshasa.

In August I did my sixth bush tour with a good friend, Pat Forbes, as my co-pilot. We were based at Mount Darwin working primarily with the RLI under the command of Major Pete Hean, another with whom I became great mates. On our first day we had to operate into the strip at Marymount Mission, close to the Mozambican border where terrorists had shot and killed some missionaries. Missionaries were a continual soft target for the terrorists because by their very calling they were unable to turn any person away from their doors. The missions were almost always staffed by young, dedicated women who were very tempting targets for terrorists to rape and subsequently kill. Based on published and publicly available records, terrorists murdered—often brutally—more than 80 unarmed and defenceless missionaries and their families.

Marymount had a very short landing strip, right on the limits of the length into which we could operate the Dakota. An additional, complicating factor was that the strip sloped steeply from west to east, so our *modus operandi* was always to land uphill and take off downhill, which made operating into Marymount relatively straightforward. That was the case on our first day. However, the next day when we had to return to the mission, the wind was well over 20 knots from the east, denying us a safe landing uphill. Pat was in charge of the sector and we came to the same conclusion that we would have to land downhill, but into the strong wind. The missionaries, knowing that aircraft never regularly landed downhill, had planted a pawpaw (papaya) plantation right next to the start of the runway. Pat knew that he would have to touch down absolutely at the runway's threshold. He declared that the pawpaw trees would not hinder his approach. I concurred.

During the final stage of the approach, we could hear the trees banging and scraping the underside of the aircraft. Once we had landed and were taxiing back up the hill, we could see a perfect profile of the Dakota cut into the plantation. The undercarriage had collected a few branches and leaves but had sustained no damage.

During our time there we undertook two cross border resupply operations, one into Zambia and the second a resupply to the SAS very close to the Cabora Bassa (now Cahora Bassa) dam. We were also involved in many fireforce callouts and I believe we set a Rhodesian war record—and probably a world landmark—of parachuting the same troops into combat three times in one day.

Towards the end of our bush tour at Mt Darwin we decided we needed a break as we had been constantly at war for days. With the local situation quiet for the moment, we hatched a plan with Pete Hean who suggested there may be a need to deploy the aircraft overnight to Centenary because there were reports of a terrorist presence there. We flew into Centenary at last light, secured the aircraft and then drove to Pat's farm which was close by and had a fabulous evening with Cally Forbes, Pat's wife, enjoying a *braaivleis* (barbecue) and several beers. We had the aircraft back to Darwin by first light the next morning, all ready for hostilities, which luckily did not materialise until later in the day.

September was another busy month with a callup for my seventh bush tour based at Mtoko. We were involved in two fireforce callouts, dropping our paratroops on both occasions with the successful result of 11 terrorists killed. The end of the month and early October found Gus Tattersall and me on another series of Air France charters that took us to Abu Dhabi, Niamey (Niger), Ndjamena (Chad), Baghdad, (Iraq), Brazzaville (Congo), and Brussels and Ostend in Belgium. Later in the month I did much the same series of flights with Mike Gibson but managing to fly into Hamburg (Germany) as well. By now the workload was ramping up in both organisations and I was flying nearly every day, either for the air force or Affretair/Cargoman.

December was frantic too; I flew more than 120 hours in the month. Mid-month I started my eighth bush tour, this time based at Chiredzi. We were busy during the day, and almost every night flew resupply sorties to the SAS across the border, often in extremely poor weather and low cloud, making for the toughest and most dangerous flying possible. During the seven days on tour we completed more than 30 daylight hours of flying and an additional 15 at night.

The SAS had set up a base at Mabalauta in the remote Gonarezhou National Park about 30 kilometres from the Mozambican border town of Malvernia. Since most of our time involved working with the SAS, we flew in and out of the strip many times. The approach into the base in a fixed wing aircraft demanded flying an angled approach until you passed a large tree indicating the centreline of the strip. You could then align yourself on short final for the landing.

On one sortie, we loaded up a team of SAS paratroops under the command of of the soon-to-be legend, Major Grahame Wilson. We flew them over the most inhospitable terrain, miles and miles of marshland, until we could glimpse the Mozambique Channel near Lourenco Marques (now Maputo). By now, we were at their ideal HALO drop altitude of about 13,000 to 14,000 feet above sea level, whereupon they exited the aircraft following their box of weapons, ammunition, and supplies down. Predawn some days later we took off to land at Mabalauta at first light before setting off in formation with choppers on a mission to recover the SAS troops we had dropped days previously.

Because we had also been resupplying other units at night, sleep was in short supply. Perhaps I was not concentrating as intensely as I should have been. It's also possible I had become accustomed to the tree on our final approach into Mabalauta and believed I would manage to just miss it prior to landing. Wrong.

On short final we heard and felt a substantial thump and once we had landed, we noticed a good portion of the starboard wingtip had been ripped off, with shards of aluminium protruding at the end of the wing. The base commander wanted to ground the aircraft immediately, but I knew the Dakota would still fly perfectly well. I persuaded the technicians on the ground to hacksaw off the jagged shreds and use helicopter blade tape to seal the exposed cavity, and we set off after a couple of hours' delay. Two helicopters would lead the formation with a ground attack aircraft in attendance in case of enemy action. We would follow in the Dakota with spare fuel to replenish the helicopters which, with the pickup of Wilson and his men, put their flight beyond the range of a single tank of fuel.

That one wing was now a few feet shorter than the other was scarcely noticeable and the Dak flew beautifully, as always. We had no maps of the area to aid navigation. We flew back across miles of marshland and vast expanses of standing water dotted with the occasional small, dry island. It was a case of maintaining a steady heading and hoping that at the end of three hours' flying, the choppers would find a small group of soldiers.

Fortune favoured us; they arrived spot on target and uplifted the troops. Soon after they found some dry ground and we dropped two drums of fuel. The choppers, heavier with their extra human load, needed two more refuelling stops. On the first two halts the choppers had kept their engines running but by the third stop, the crews and SAS personnel felt in need of a leg stretch, so they shut down while they refuelled. Alarmingly, one chopper's engine refused to start; the igniter had failed. We circled overhead while the pilots on the ground debated tactics. By this time the ground attack aircraft had returned to base, pleading a fuel shortage of his own. We also speculated that a lack of action and subsequent boredom might have contributed to his departure. Base radioed us to return and collect a spare igniter pack. Before leaving, we took a close look at the choppers resting place, a tiny island in the middle of what seem like limitless, watery marsh-land. Could we relocate them on our return?

The problem worsened. Contacting base, we learned that the only spare readily available was back at New Sarum (Salisbury). We kept to our original heading until we crossed a river and established a definite starting point for our return trip. From there we could turn north and head for base and the spare part.

Once home, we quickly refuelled, quelling the horror of the ground technicians. They could not believe we would continue our mission in one of their beloved Dakotas with one wing shorter than the other. We collected the spare, packaged in a small box which we would have to throw out of the aircraft, landing it close to the choppers rather than into the water. No-one thought to give us two igniters in case we messed up dropping the first. How often hindsight embarrassed us.

We found our river crossing point and took up our original heading, praying we would find our two helicopters. Again, fortune favoured our navigation and we spotted them at our first attempt. While waiting for our return, Graham and his entourage—hungry, having not eaten a proper meal for days—felt secure enough to shoot a buck, light a fire, and initiate a *braaivleis*, or barbecue. Not only did it satisfy their hunger, it gave me smoke as a wind indicator. I decided to fly as low as I could before commanding the dispatcher to deposit the box, hoping the wind would not interfere with my calculations for the drop. Taking a deep breath, I started my run towards the choppers and when I thought the box would land in the right place, I gave the order 'green light on'. Of course, I couldn't see the results of my 'bombing' run, but soon I heard an exclamation over the radio from the ground that the box had landed between two of the chopper's blades. The consequences of the box hitting a blade, or a chopper, or even a person were unthinkable, but as far as I was concerned, I didn't care as long as the box landed on dry ground and not in the water.

I circled overhead until they got the engine started, then escorted them across the border before setting course back to Chiredzi. No rest for us though. We had to complete our day job ferrying troops and supplies to Fort Victoria and Thornhill before returning to New Sarum to have the aircraft repaired. It was an eventful and in parts nerve-wracking day during which we had been airborne for more than 11 hours.

As a sequel to my wing-clipping incident, the SAS detachment at Mabalauta decided that a tree should not stand in the way of a simple landing at the strip. In their efficient, no-nonsense way, they ringed the innocent tree with a generous selection of explosives and blew it out of the ground. The next time I flew into Mabalauta, starkly visible on the final approach was a volcanic crater where the unhappy tree once stood. I admit I felt a blend of relief and guilt. It would cause no more flying anxiety, but it was a magnificent specimen.

As the year closed, I reflected on more than a 1,000 flying hours in 11 months—a heavy workload in those days, though necessary for the times. And I was still alive.

CHAPTER 14

Pseudo ops, contraband, and death of a Viscount—1978

January

In early January, I had to fly to an airstrip in the south east of the country, where I was to position the Dakota as close to the tree line as possible from which we could take off with minimum taxi time. Orders were to wait inside the aircraft with the door closed. Eventually a truck arrived and reversed up to the door. A canvas canopy covered the rear of the vehicle as well as our door, precluding anyone outside seeing who or what entered the aircraft.

The stench from the back of the truck was overpowering as they lifted the canopy to allow the occupants of the truck to file across onto the aircraft. It looked like a dozen black terrorists—the very enemy with whom we were locked in deadly combat—had just had just boarded my aircraft. They all carried AK-47s, the automatic assault rifle favoured by the terrorists, and obviously they had not washed for weeks. As I walked up the aisle to the cockpit having secured the door and completed my internal checks before take-off, a strangely-

European voice from the black ranks said. 'Hi Ian.' I looked closer at the black face addressing me and saw with a jolt of surprise that his eyes were a piercing blue.

Only then, beneath the smudged black camouflage cream, I recognised Dennis Croukamp, an old friend. I had not seen him for years; not since we were lads together at Kamativi where he was known as Dennis Moodie. The Moodies had taken him in as a foster child, but later in life he resumed his birth surname, Croukamp.

And who should be next to him, a grin etched on his blackened face, but Neil Kriel. Neil had usefully advised me to shorten my stride as I overtook him at an inter school cross country event 12 or 13 years ago. He was the same boy who ran clean through me as I tried to tackle him in a rugby match against Umtali Boys' High school two years later. Both were well established and highly decorated members of the Selous Scouts, Rhodesia's clandestine reconnaissance and combat unit.

The scouts were noted for their bush and tracking skills, endurance, and fearless temperament. According to subsequent military intelligence, they were responsible for 68 per cent of all terrorist deaths within the country for the duration of the war. Croukamp's and Kriel's colleagues on the truck were captured terrorists whom the army and particularly Special Branch had 'turned'. They now belonged to the Selous Scouts family, and were part of what was termed pseudo-operations. Most captured terrorists faced execution by hanging or long prison terms. Some were given the option of joining the scouts. While a few deserted and returned to the terrorists' ranks, the great majority became loyal and valuable Selous Scout soldiers. After our brief but delighted exchange, I flew them back to their base at Andre Rabie barracks.

The busy month saw me fly nearly one hundred hours, adding Bangui (Central African Republic), Salalah (Oman), Mvengue (Gabon), Windhoek (South West Africa) and Las Palmas (Canary Isles) to my itinerary of visited airports. At its end, flying with Sam Richman, we took off at sunrise from Amsterdam and arrived at Salisbury at sunrise three days later, having flown without a break to Baghdad, Abu Dhabi, Muscat, and finally to Salisbury. Having landed at Muscat, and expecting a night stop, we received an urgent message from the Boss asking if we would consider bringing the aircraft back immediately; an urgent requirement for another charter had come up unexpectedly. Eight hours later as the sun crept over the horizon we landed back at base, where Malloch came out to the aircraft to thanks us personally.

February 1 marked the start of my ninth bush tour, positioned again out of Chiredzi. My co-pilot was another former World War Two pilot who had volunteered to do his callups with the air force. Our primary task, apart from the routine transport assignments for the Dakota, was to resupply the SAS and Selous Scouts operating across the border in Mozambique in the south of the country. On the first night, after a successful resupply flight, we came unwittingly close to the Mozambican town of Malvernia, heavily fortified with anti-aircraft weaponry. We came under intense fire for a time but took hasty evasive action. Luckily, we sustained no hits or damage. The next morning, I woke to find my co-pilot roommate in a frightful state, shaking, bleary-eyed, and sleepless since our return. The flak we experienced the previous evening had rekindled nightmares of similar episodes during the European war and he felt incapable of continuing. I felt dreadfully sorry for him, having heard horror tales from other, older pilots. I embraced him as sympathetically as I could, and quickly arranged for his return to Salisbury on the Air Rhodesia Viscount. I spoke confidentially to our CO on his arrival back at the squadron. I am glad air force command handled his case gently and with empathy, allowing him to return quietly to civilian life.

On my return to the squadron, I received a word of thanks for my handling of the situation, balanced by an admonishment for hitting the tree and taking a chunk out of the Dakota's wing in December. In retrospect, it was more of a slap with a feather. The incident was closed, with the acknowledgement that mishaps occur on operations, and that I should be more careful in the future. 'Yes sir, point taken, and thank you.'

Our daily duty on the Dakota was to shuttle supplies, troops, and pilots between the FAFs. To avoid small arms fire, or worse, we mostly flew at treetop level between the airfields which were never that far apart, certainly not distant enough to warrant climbing to a safe height before setting course. We would only climb to an economic cruising altitude between major aerodromes on flights of about an hour, more or less. Fifty feet above the ground or trees was our aim. Poor helicopter pilots or other air crew on repositioning flights in the back of the aircraft hated every second of their journey as they watched trees higher than the aircraft passing by the window. Some would have recently seen combat and survived. No doubt they held the pessimistic but private view that if the war didn't kill them, the lunatics from 3 Squadron would. Any height beyond 100 feet above ground level was considered hazardous, improving the opportunities for terrorists to put up fire with increasingly dangerous weapons.

March

On March 8 I was tasked to carry out a changeover shuttle from New Sarum to Chiredzi and back via Thornhill, Shabani (now Zvishavane), and Fort Victoria (now Masvingo). At Thornhill we picked up several people who were destined to start their tours of duty at the various stops en route. My co-pilot was an ex-United States Air Force Vietnam veteran with a chest full of medals on his number one uniform. I assigned him the sector between Fort Victoria and Chiredzi. The terrain between the two was more hilly than flat, but in my opinion, you could still pick your way close to the ground.

When a colleague has the controls, I prefer to keep intrusion to a minimum, especially as this was the first time I had flown with this newcomer to the squadron. However, my discomfort mounted as he chose to fly at about 200 feet on a route between two sets of hills, slightly taller on each side than our own height. I was about to voice my concerns, to drop altitude, and to steer a course around the hills, not between them. Too late. We flew into a storm of fire from the slopes on both sides, a ground-mounted aerial ambush.

I was grateful our assailants appeared to lack RPGs or we would have been at serious if not potentially fatal risk. We had a dozen passengers in the back of the aircraft and we soon smelled cordite and saw whisps of smoke in the passenger compartment. I grabbed the controls, dived the plane, and levelled out just above the trees. As soon as we were clear and the firing had stopped, I gave him back control of the aircraft so I could transmit our position to Chiredzi to deploy a ground attack aircraft. Caught by surprise, my brain (and my arse) briefly locked up and I could not focus swiftly enough on reporting our loc-stat, the map coordinates capturing our exact position. By the time I had sorted out where we were it was too late to send a response aircraft; the terrorists would have dispersed. The moment we landed we assessed the damage. Mercifully no-one was hit. Glob, a regular air force officer seated in the back, had bullet holes either side of him. Had we been carrying a technician in the cockpit, he would have taken a bullet up his backside—a round had burst straight through the jump seat. Another bullet grazed the back of my seat, missing me by inches. Although the attack caused no structural or operational damage to the aircraft, the techs counted a total of 64 holes in the fuselage. Curiously, our American friend left the squadron soon after.

The political situation in Rhodesia continued to deteriorate. White-hall maintained its pressure. A decade and more before, secret but unproductive meetings had taken place between Ian Smith and Harold Wilson, the British Prime Minister aboard the Royal Navy ships HMS *Tiger* in 1966 and HMS *Fearless* in 1968. In 1975, at the initiative of South African President, John Forster, and co-mediator, President Kenneth Kaunda of Zambia, further talks took place with the South African and Zambian presidents, as well as representatives of Bishop Abel Muzorewa's UANC, and ZANU and ZAPU on the Victoria Falls bridge. The conference was abandoned after a day with none of the sides reaching any agreement. A further conference was convened in Geneva as a result of the US Secretary of State Henry Kissinger putting pressure on South Africa to have Ian Smith agree to majority rule within two years. Backed into a corner by his powerful ally, Smith reluctantly agreed. He signed an accord with Muzorewa. Both terrorist organisations consented to a ceasefire but never adhered to the agreement. The war not only continued, but intensified.

To make things worse, Portugal had ceded Angola and Mozambique to nationalist governments which committed themselves to the downfall of the Rhodesian government by actively aiding both terrorist organisations. South Africa was less helpful than previously because it was trying to relieve pressure from its anti-apartheid opponents throughout the world. Affretair had regularly flown cargoes of meat into Greece but a change in government there brought a halt to that outlet and resulted in jail for the import agent.

The United Nations Security Council had endorsed universal sanctions against Rhodesia and through the ongoing complaints of the Organisation of African Unity (OAU), continual pressure was levied on all countries to ban entry or overflight by Air Gabon Cargo or Cargoman. However, despite the difficulties, we still consistently flew meat into Gabon, the Ivory Coast, Nigeria, Holland, Switzerland, and the Comoros Islands, among other countries. We flew into France regularly to pick up spares for the Rheims ground attack aircraft as well as the Aerospatiale helicopters, and into Oman to collect Hawker Hunter aircraft spares. Angola and Zambia now prohibited overflight. On all fronts, militarily, politically, and eco-nomically, the noose around the Rhodesian neck tightened further, but no side considered a surrender. Sadly, marauding terrorist groups—effectively little more than undisciplined armed bandits—massacred more and more innocent people within the country. Their brutality turned the population against the government. Fear breeds insecurity and much of the black, rural population was now more scared of upsetting the insurgents than supporting those who strove to protect their lives.

I was under no illusion that our time was limited and would on occasions have heated discussions with Jerry and other friends. My problem, and my opinion still, was that unlike Britain during the Second World War, I did not believe our population as a whole was totally committed to the war. To some it appeared more of a game with the naïve belief that we would win in the end. To me in the mid nineteen seventies, Rhodesia's demise was inevitable, despite the magnificent and generally successful military campaigns. In my opinion, we were doomed economically and politically. My frustration lay with how to end the conflict with some dignity and honour before more superbly brave people died. None seemed to be forthcoming, with little collective intelligence being applied by those in power or those making so-called important decisions.

Late in March I undertook another callup mainly resupplying the SAS, again across the border in Mozambique near Chipinga (now Chipinge).

On the last day of the month, we added a new destination to which we delivered meat, Basel in Switzerland. Soon we would be flying into Zurich, delivering a similar cargo.

The flights from Salisbury to Libreville lengthened because we could no longer fly directly over Zambia and Angola. We knew Cuban pilots were flying Soviet-built, Angola-based MiG fighter aircraft, and calculated that if we cut a corner over western Angola, even if they scrambled immediately, they could not catch us before we reached neutral territory over the Atlantic. We used the tactic on many flights to Libreville, reducing flying time and fuel consumption.

On the morning of March 24, Tom Phillips, a former World War Two pilot and a captain on our CL-44 aircraft, decided he would chance the short cut since there were several differing cloud layers over southern Angola. As a turbo prop aircraft, the CL-44 flew at much lower altitudes than the DC-8, making it far more vulnerable to interception, which is exactly what happened as he came out of a layer of cloud.

Three MiGs had formatted on him and even fired a salvo of rockets over the cockpit roof to ensure he followed them into their base at Huambo. Tom, a canny and experienced pilot, slowed the aircraft down as much as possible, making it more difficult for the jets to maintain formation with him. On the final approach into Huambo, he applied full power, raised the flaps and flew at extremely low level directly towards the range of hills to the south where he was able to evade his interceptors.

Mike Gibson and I were returning from Libreville when our base contacted us. They knew of the interception but had lost high frequency radio contact (HF). Could we clarify the situation, and render help if needed? We turned south across Angola and eventually made VHF radio contact with them to learn that although they were still over Angolan territory, they were safe for the moment. Soon after they radioed to say they had crossed the Angola/South West Africa border and were heading to Windhoek as they lacked sufficient fuel to return to base or reach Port Gentil in Gabon, their destination. It was a disaster averted. We dared not imagine what would have become of the crew if they had landed at Huambo and been imprisoned, which would have been inevitable.

The incident gave me an insight. We were heavy on the outbound journey to Libreville and therefore restricted to altitudes of between 31,000 and 35,000 feet. We had little option but to take the long out-to-sea route. But, on the return journey, we were so light we could climb to 40,000 feet, or higher. The Cuban-piloted MiGs, however, had a limited range, so when I became a captain I would fly directly back to Salisbury over Angola and Zambia knowing that the MiGs would struggle to catch us even if they became airborne as soon as they knew we had entered their airspace. Others I knew did the same.

We would have previously filed a flight plan that took us over the longer route and would transmit false crossing times of the various waypoints involved. In reality we were several hundred miles away from where we said we were.

There were no MiGs based in Mozambique as yet. When we flew to the Seychelles or up to Oman, we would take off from Salisbury and fly straight across Mozambique without breaking radio silence until we were in range of Moroni on the Comoros Isles. We would then ask them to initiate a flight plan as if Moroni was our departure point, with a departure time adjusted to validate our deception. In contravention of the international laws of aviation, we would switch on our navigation lights and rotating beacon only at night. They always remained off if we were flying over hostile territory. We would also fly at non-standard levels. The traffic collision avoidance system (TCAS) had not yet been invented. Ignorance was bliss.

June

In June we ran a number of charters to Argentina, as well as several air force missions. With my two Atlantic crossings to Buenos Aires and back, I completed a journey up to Abu Dhabi and Muscat via the Seychelles. They added up to an impressive 130 hours flying in the month on top of two simulator checks.

July

July was another busy month with just as much flying. On July 26 I was Boss Jack's co-pilot on the first of many 'smersh' missions. In our case smersh meant clandestine sorties. We borrowed the description from the James Bond novels and fictional films based on the real life World War Two Soviet counter-intelligence unit, SMERSH. Our smersh sorties were to help either the South Africans or Angola's opposition guerrilla movement, UNITA, under Jonas Savimbi. UNITA, with support from South Africa, the US, and the CIA, wanted to depose their former comrades in the Angolan independence struggle, the Marxist MPLA government.

We flew from Salisbury to Libreville, ferrying a shipment of arms from the Gabonese capital into Kamina, the principal military base in the Democratic Republic of the Congo (DRC). The DRC was also training some of the UNITA troops and over a hundred personnel and their equipment would make up our return load. As a military airfield in the middle of a relatively poor African country, it had none of the usual aviation aids such as visual approach slope indicators (VASIs) or instrument landing system technology (ILS) to assist our landing.

We termed it a 'black hole' approach. With the sensitivity of the operation, the flight tower controllers switched on the runway lights only when they judged we had entered our final approach. It was a chicken-or-egg, touch-and-go equation. Without any standard aids to guide us, how could we know accurately whether it was our final approach or not? Captain Jack was in charge of the sector. Once he had aligned the aircraft on the runway centreline, he decided the best way to determine his approach path angle was to dive until he had the grass visual in the landing lights. He then flew level until we were over the runway threshold, closed the throttles, and plonked the aircraft down on the runway. It was, a novel, unusual, and nerve-wracking method of landing a large four-engine jet in the dark onto unfamiliar terrain.

Ground crew wheeled in steps to unload the shipment of arms and re-load the empty cargo hold with troops. As a freighter, we had no passenger seats, so we instructed the trainees to find whatever space they could on the floor. The DC-8s of that era had no auxiliary power unit (APU), a self-supporting means of starting the aircraft engines. It needed an independent ground power unit (GPU) to provide enough air to turn the fan and turbine blades to a sufficient speed so that the first engine would start. Kamina, as a military jet fighter base, had no compatible GPU for an aircraft like ours. We had to carry our own unit, strapped onto a pallet close to the cargo door.

When we were ready to start an engine, we fired up the GPU, which is basically a small jet engine itself. The noise throughout the aircraft and especially the cockpit was phenomenal and probably terrifying for our passengers, many of whom would never have flown in their lives, let alone on a monstrous beast like ours. We had to work through all the pre-start checks beforehand and then complete the start procedure using hand signals as we could not hear each other speak. Once one engine was successfully running, we could shut down the GPU, close the cargo hatch, and ignite the remaining three engines from the power of the first.

We had carefully planned our arrival time into Kamina for nightfall and departure well before dawn, a point on which Malloch was adamant. We then flew the trainees to Grootfontein, a South African military base which they had established in South West Africa (now Namibia). The troops would then tranship into Angola to re-join the UNITA forces. Mission accomplished, we returned directly to Salisbury.

Days after our return we had orders to attend an evening briefing at New Sarum followed by a night lockdown for security reasons. Military intelligence believed a camp at Tembue-2 in Mozambique, north of the Cabora Bassa dam, could contain as many as 3,000 terrorists. ComOps planned a mass attack at 0800 the next morning, July 30.

Apart from the ground attack aircraft and fireforce choppers which had prepositioned close to the border already, eight Dakotas each containing 24 paratroopers from all para-trained army units got airborne. We set off in formation until approaching the target area where we split up to despatch our troops into the drop zones designated to us. I was in formation behind another Dakota and when he had dropped his troops, I would then drop ours with the intention of forming stop and sweep lines at each side and end of the camps. It now appeared there were many small camps, so the strategy was to effectively close the sides of a box around them. The drop was uneventful, and we subsequently returned to Chiswiti, from where we flew several fuel resupply drops to the helicopters operating in the area during the rest of the day.

However, the whole operation was a disaster from start to finish. There was apparently not just one camp containing 3,000 terrorists, but many smaller makeshift hutted areas containing hundreds more. Communications had failed because of incompatible radio frequencies between the air force and Captain Chris 'Schulie' Schulenberg, legendary Selous Scouts recce specialist who had been dropped in many days before. The drop zones had been changed without alerting the Dakotas, which consequently deployed their troops in the wrong place. Much finger pointing and blaming took place in the days after the abortive raid. I spent the next two days flying in and out of the area resupplying the helicopters. They were trying to help track down terrorists who had dispersed when they saw the paratroops drop some distance from their camps, as well as uplifting SAS troops who had completed their mop up missions.

On one of the days, we were waiting for troops to be helicoptered back from across the border. The conditions were dusty, so my co-pilot decided to put protective covers back on the pitot tubes (devices providing a pressure differential that fed the altimeter and air speed indicator). Once we were fully uploaded with troops and it was time to depart, we started up and taxied to the end of the short strip for take-off. Halfway down the runway, when it was too late to abort, I realised we had no airspeed indication. My companion was mortified when he realised he had forgotten to retrieve the pitot cover before departure, which meant we had no height readout either. I decided we had to come back and land, so I had no option but to fly a circuit based on instinct and memory as to attitude and power settings. In the end we landed successfully and taxied back to the top of the runway. My co-pilot suffered the blushing ignominy of negotiating his way through the bemused soldiers, opening the door, lowering the steps and retrieving the pitot cover, before returning to the cockpit. I felt for him. The troops gave him a ribbing on his way back.

August

Colonel Bob Dinard had now temporarily established himself in the Comoros Islands and in August, I flew two trips with Boss Jack into Moroni where he caught up with Dinard while we were on the ground. We followed up with a third in September.

September

Late in the afternoon of Sunday September 3., Flight 825, an Air Rhodesia Viscount laden with tourists and holiday-makers with a total of 56 on board, took off from Kariba on its return to Salisbury. Soon after take-off a heat seeking missile slammed into the aircraft, taking out both starboard engines. Struggling to manoeuvre, the pilots managed a near-miraculous controlled crash into an area of clear ground. Luck turned further against them. The aircraft bellied into a large ditch, causing it to cartwheel and burst into flames. Of the 56 people aboard, 38 died in the crash, including the two pilots, Captain John Hood and First Officer Garth Beaumont. Beaumont had just resigned from Air Rhodesia and was about to start a DC-8 course with Affretair. Ten of the survivors, including the two air hostesses, Dulcie Esterhuizen and Louise Pearson, stayed with the survivors and the aircraft while eight others went to look for help and water. A group of terrorists arrived soon after, indicated they had come to help, but rounded up the helpless and traumatised group and shot them all as well as bayoneting to death a three-week-old baby and its mother.

During the night the air force undertook a series of flights trying unsuccessfully to find the crash site. A team of SAS soldiers took to the air at first light in a Dakota which spent hours searching the likely area. I received a call that night, taking orders to deliver a taskforce of paratroops to Kariba and stand by. The whole country was in a state of shock, because no one yet knew the fate of the Viscount whose final distress call remained the sole clue to the impending disaster.

We endured some tough hours. Kariba town and airport are small and by now hundreds of people had gathered anxiously, including the desperate relatives and friends of the missing passengers, all wanting information. I found it too harrowing to stay in the terminal, instead choosing to remain with the aircraft outside on the apron. A photograph appeared in the Rhodesia Herald newspaper the next day with me obviously showing signs of the strain, talking to one of the anxiously waiting relatives.

Soon after midday we received news that security forces had located the crash site. We got airborne immediately, found the position, and dropped our troops near the shockingly visible wreckage. Only then, via radio from the SAS troops on the ground, we learned the full horror of what had transpired. Such were my flying commitments at the time, I had little time to reflect. The next day I was in the DC-8 on a round trip to Libreville. It was a grim period, but we were not to know that darker days still lay ahead.

ATA had now 'loaned' its DC-7 to the Rhodesian Air Force which had already used it on successful cross border operations dropping paratroops and fuel. As these were now military rather than civil operations, only a small nucleus of military approved pilots was used. Generally Boss Jack was the commander, but at times Colin Miller (ex RhAF), our chief pilot, would command the flight. George Alexander, our 3 Squadron CO, and Jerry Lynch had converted onto the aircraft and were the primary co-pilots and John Matthews and I were chosen as standby, should Jerry or George be unavailable.

The day before I flew to Moroni with Boss Jack, I was rostered to fly as Colin's co-pilot on the DC-7 from New Sarum to Bloemfontein in South Africa and from there to Waterkloof, a South African Air Force base near Pretoria, and back to New Sarum. It was an exhilarating day; in all my fantasies, I never believed I would get to fly such an iconic aircraft.

Flying the DC-7 was completely different from operating the DC-3 or DC-8, in that the flight engineer was the primary task master. He raised the undercarriage, raised and lowered the flaps at the pilot's command, and controlled the power levers throughout. The pilot, during landing approaches, would simply ask for so many inches of thrust which the flight engineer would duly provide. All the pilot controlled, in effect, was the stick or control column.

Our orders were to deliver ordnance to Bloemfontein and then collect a consignment of military hardware and weapons from Waterkloof, which we accomplished without incident, though we stirred up a level of curiosity introducing this large, antiquated aircraft into a sophisticated military base.

For the remainder of September and into October, while continuing with military missions, I was also heavily engaged on the DC-8 flying to Gabon and the Congo as well as new destinations, Sharjah, Luxembourg, and Malta.

October

At this stage, terrorists in ever increasing numbers undertook training in both Zambia and Mozambique. This, and the downing of the Viscount, gave rise to widespread and vocal calls for reprisal attacks across the borders, taking the fight to the insurgents.

Aerial reconnaissance had established the presence of three large camps in Zambia containing an estimated 4,000 terrorists under training. Before any possible deployment into Rhodesia, ComOps decided to attack all three on the same day, October 19. The first objective was the main base, Chikumbi, or Freedom camp at Westlands Farm about 10 miles from the capital, Lusaka. Canberra bombers would initiate the attack, followed by a strike force of Hunters, closely followed by helicopter gunships to supposedly mop up.

The personnel of each camp always paraded at 0830 every day. At exactly that time the bombing attack went in with both sets of aircraft dropping their bombs accurately and successfully. The camp, however, was strongly defended with sophisticated and heavy anti-aircraft weaponry which hit a ground attack aircraft, forcing it to withdraw. Ground fire also shot down one of the four helicopter gunships, seriously injuring the pilot and gunner, though both survived.

The Zambian Air Force Base at Mumbwa, 93 miles to the west of Lusaka, had both MiG 17 and MiG 19 fighters, with which the Rhodesian Air Force had no wish to engage. Once he had dropped his bombs on the camp, the lead aircraft of Green section of the Canberra bomber force (Green Leader), contacted the air traffic control tower at Lusaka airport. Squadron Leader Chris Dixon informed them that the attack was against Rhodesian dissidents at Westlands Farm and not against Zambia or her security forces. He added that as Rhodesian Air Force fighters were circling over Mumbwa, any Zambian fighter sent up to retaliate would be shot down and all air traffic into and out of Lusaka airport was suspended until further notice. The recording of the exchange with the Lusaka tower is immortalised as the Green Leader tape, available on YouTube or similar podcasts.

The second camp, at Mkushi, about 77 miles to the north east of Lusaka, would be attacked soon afterwards. At 1145 the Canberra bombers, having re-armed after the earlier raid, dropped their bombs on the camp followed immediately by a bombing run by a section of Hunters. Six Dakotas with 20 SAS paratroops each would drop their troops immediately after the airstrikes went in. I was in command of one of the Daks. We had taken off from Salisbury earlier, flown over the Cabora Bassa dam, and crossed into Zambia from the south flying at very low level, which was miserably uncomfortable for the troops in the back. Approaching the target, we could see the smoke from the air strike and each aircraft turned to drop their troops adjacent to the camp. Some of the troops were dropped marginally too close to the action and were immediately involved in a contact before they could properly organise into a sweep line. Sadly, a female terrorist mortally wounded one trooper from my aircraft, the first time our troops had encountered female dissident fighters.

HEADWIND: AN AFRICAN AIR ODYSSEY

We were based at Kariba for the next few days and flew several fuel resupply missions, mainly to Rufunsa which the Rhodesians had secured as a refuelling stop for the helicopters. Rufunsa was very close to the third camp (CGT 2) that was attacked that day. However, by the time the strike force arrived the camp was deserted, having been alerted as a result of the other strikes. Nevertheless, our troops remained in Zambia for some time with support from the helicopters which we kept fuelled.

The Mkushi camp was very well constructed with considerable evidence of a Russian presence. Our resupply runs into Zambia were vital, and on a resupply mission one afternoon we had the reassuring presence of two Hunters escorting us in case the Zambians scrambled their MiG's to find us. As our forward speed was so much slower than the Hunters, they flew an oval shaped pattern keeping us in the middle as we trundled to our destination.

Red One was another great friend. Malcolm 'Baldy' Baldwin later informed me that he had received information that a MiG had just got airborne and that as he was running short of fuel, we were now on our own. 'Thanks, Baldy.'

We flew at treetop height until we dropped off our fuel load, knowing that if the MiG was looking for us it would probably find it impossible to spot our camouflaged Dak at such a low level. In the end it was an uneventful sortie and we returned successfully to Kariba.

The next day we were on another resupply run and I had given the sector to my co-pilot who chose to return at a relatively high altitude hoping any heat-seeking anti-aircraft missile would lock onto a cloud rather than our exhaust. Slightly bemused, I did not override his decision. On our return journey a large anti-aircraft battery over which we had flown opened up on us. My pilot colleague correctly turned at right angles from our course and dived the aircraft towards the ground while I tried to establish from where the fire was coming. The aircraft started to shake and vibrate which prompted me to check our instruments. The airspeed indicator (ASI) was accelerating through a speed of 220 knots. The never-exceed speed (VNE) of the Dakota was normally 206 knots but we were restricted to 193 knots because we now had anti-Strela ground-to-air missile tubes fitted to diffuse our exhaust gases. I gently closed the throttles and as calmly as I could asked him if we could slow down, with which he too examined the instruments, muttered an expletive, and started pulling on the control column to reduce speed. Fortunately, I anticipated his reaction and used my knee to block the rearward movement of the column because any sudden G-force could have caused possibly severe structural damage. We soon resumed normal flight and exited the flak emplacement's range of fire, undamaged but shaken.

On my return to Salisbury, I was quickly off again in the DC-8 on a trip absorbing the rest of the month, racking up a total of 125 hours flown during October. No wonder my private life started to creak. I was hardly ever at home.

November

Air Rhodesia had also loaned the air force a civilian Dakota, VP-YNH, which although painted in camouflage colours and looking for the world like a military aircraft, retained its forward-facing civilian seats. This allowed us to transport passengers in relative comfort. On November 7 I was privileged to fly a team of SAS soldiers under the command of Captain Grahame Wilson to Langebaan, a military base close to Cape Town in South Africa.

The Dak's limited range was an issue, forcing us to fly stages from New Sarum to Waterkloof, near Pretoria, and from there to Langebaan. As the total flight time was nearly 10 hours, we enjoyed several conversations en route with Wilson and his team. As always with the need-to-know policy, we were not informed of the nature of their mission. I subsequently learned Grahame was to lead an assault on ZANU leader, Robert Mugabe's house in Maputo, with deployment from Cape Town by submarine. We spent the night at Langebaan in a deserted officers' mess and returned the next day via Waterkloof.

Later in the month I flew with Sam Richman on a new route from Salisbury to the Comoros Islands where we off-loaded a cargo of meat before moving on to Mombasa and from there to Sanaa in Yemen for the night. It was a curious journey from the airport to our hotel. The army controlled the poorly lit city throughout the hours of darkness, requiring us to halt at several roadblocks manned by soldiers all armed with Kalashnikov machine guns. Returning the next morning, not only had all the roadblocks and soldiers disappeared but with daylight the place resembled something from ancient biblical times. The buildings were all mud-coloured low rise dwellings with flat rooves and everything appeared to be covered in grey-brown dust. No scrap of green vegetation was visible.

From Sanaa we flew to Amman before night stopping back in Muscat. Two days later we flew to Abu Dhabi and Dubai before progressing to Amsterdam where we all had to undergo our regulatory simulator checks.

December

Cargoman had earned a reputation as a trusted freight cargo charter airline in the Middle East. Over the past year the Rhodesian Cold Storage Commission, the state owned livestock slaughter and meat distribution enterprise, had managed to come to an arrangement with beef suppliers in Botswana. The arrangement let us export beef that came not only from Botswana but was supplemented with Rhodesian beef for sale to many centres in the Middle East. So on December 1, again with Sam Richman, we flew from Salisbury, to Moroni in the Comoros Islands, to Mombasa, and then a landing in Jeddah (Saudi Arabia) where we off-loaded before returning directly to Salisbury. Although we flight-planned to the Comoros Islands, we changed our destination once in radio contact with Moroni. It made for a long duty day with more than 13 hours airborne combined with all the ground time. I undertook another similar operation with Roger Brackley two weeks later, punctuated with several beef export expeditions to Brazzaville in the DRC.

On December 6 I began another weeklong bush tour based at Chiredzi with Mike Cappucitti. We were occupied every day with resupply flights, fireforce callouts, and at night, resupply missions to the SAS in Mozambique, which made it an exhausting week. Every fireforce callout resulted in us dropping troops into contact situations. On one callout we were circling while the helicopters tried to establish the exact location of a group of terrorists who had scattered earlier with the approach of our fireforce. The ground attack aircraft accompanying us had to peel off to another contact and the G-car had to depart to refuel. The nearest fuel supply necessitated a round trip of at least 30 minutes, leaving us in the Dakota and the K-car flown by Chas Goatley searching the bush below us. Soon Goatley had to refuel, and we learned that our G-car had also diverted to another sighting. We feared our sortie was quickly turning into a lemon, a venture not worth pursuing.

With the G-car gone, I re-commenced the search in an ever increasing circumference away from the original sighting. The strategy paid dividends when I spotted a large group running through the bush. I immediately alerted the dispatcher that I would drop all our sticks in batches of two sticks at a time in an attempt to create stop lines around the fleeing group. We dropped all five RAR sticks as close as I dared to the group which seemed to be travelling in one direction. We soon learned that at least two sticks had joined contact almost as soon as they landed. The K-car fortunately returned to help with the remainder of the contact, resulting in the deaths of all 12 terrorists, and a bravery award recommendation for a New Zealand soldier. Goatley paid us his compliments at the subsequent debrief.

Debriefs between ground and air forces were a vital part of the bush war, and were carried out wherever possible after a contact. All aircraft commanders and the army commander would analyse the battle and make appropriate observations on the effectiveness, or otherwise, of our performance in the air. On many occasions these debriefs could be brutal. If, for instance, a ground attack pilot had failed to direct his fire accurately, or the Dak pilot had dropped his troops at the wrong moment or in the wrong place, the criticism was harsh but always accurate and fair. It was our job to support the men at the sharp end on the ground. I was lucky to have enjoyed excellent rapport with, and guidance from experienced army commanders. I was relieved that my responses to their requests, often under life-and-death stress, met with their approval.

Towards the end of our tour at Chiredzi we flew a night resupply mission to the SAS across the border into Mozambique. Chris Tucker piloting a Lynx ground attack aircraft accompanied us in loose formation. If we encountered any problems during the run in or the drop he could, if necessary, put in an attack. The run into the SAS and resupply went according to plan and without incident. As it was a clear night, we climbed to a reasonable altitude still over Mozambique while setting course for our base. Tucker radioed me to report trails of anti-aircraft fire floating up at us. It looked so pretty in the clear night I called our dispatchers up to the cockpit to experience these impressive waves of light curving towards us and then falling away behind. Suddenly the surges of illumination grew alarmingly close and what's more, exploded. We realised abruptly this was no entertaining fireworks display, but heavy duty flak. Both of us dived hastily for the deck, at the same time turning away from our track. My aircraft started an ominous banging and thumping, with the hydraulic gauge oscillating wildly from zero to maximum. I was convinced our hydraulic system had suffered flak damage and radioed for a diversion to the longest local runway, which was at Thornhill, in case we could not lower the undercarriage or flaps. The potential emergency landing organised, we set course.

My training prompted me to initiate a cause and analysis review of the hydraulics-driven systems, starting with the undercarriage, which appeared normal in both 'up' and 'locked' positions. Examining the flap system, I noticed the flaps were fully extended. Since we were flying at a speed well in excess of the limit for which the flaps were designed, they were frantically trying to blow back. On the other hand, the hydraulics dutifully obeyed orders and tried to extend them. Gravity and contradictory commands produced the banging and thumping. We raised the flaps and everything in the cockpit returned to normal. I sheepishly contacted our forward base to stand them down and apologise. I dare not contemplate what they must have thought of me.

The explanation soon became apparent. In his eagerness to witness the dazzling lightshow, and in the unfamiliar world of the cockpit, one of the dispatchers unwittingly leant on a mechanical handle, pushing it to its fully down position and extending the flaps completely. A few days later, after submitting our debrief report, ComOps summoned Tucker and me to describe the incident and the flak. Ordnance experts determined that the flak could well have come from a powerful 88mm anti-aircraft battery such as was used during World War Two.

Just before Christmas I flew with Boss Jack to Moroni in the Comoros Islands for a night stop, which provided an opportunity for Malloch to catch up with his old mercenary colleague, Colonel Bob Dinard. Co-pilot Dave Goldsmith and I enjoyed an evening in the local hotel eating fresh seafood which was not readily available in sanctions-starved Rhodesia. We reflected guiltily on one of the perks we enjoyed as pilots still in contact with the outside world. Ordering a second round, we determined to eat a share on behalf of family and friends.

On December 27 Affretair management called all senior first officers to a meeting with the chief pilot, operations manager, and training captains. They asked each of us in turn who should become the next captain on the DC-8, a position all of us valued and aspired to. I thought it was an unpleasant and unnecessary exercise. They had flown with us all, knew our strengths and weaknesses, and should easily have been able to decide who was next in the command queue. Unlike most other airlines, Affretair eschewed a seniority system and based promotion solely on merit. Despite the rancour I felt at the meeting, I was honoured and delighted to receive a call from our chief pilot, Colin Miller, naming me the next DC-8 captain, when the need arose. It crowned a tough, industrious year with just under 1,200 hours flown.

Mike Borlace

While this is definitively Mike's story to tell it deserves some attention here because of my and my family's involvement.

During his flying training at Dartmouth my great friend, Nick Taylor, found another comrade in arms in Mike Borlace. He left the Royal Navy before his short term commission was complete but embarked upon a military career characterised by a pronounced opposition to 'the bad guys' whoever and wherever they may have been. He did a stint with the Israelis during the 1973 Yom Kippur War before coming to Rhodesia as a contract helicopter pilot. He quickly established himself as an ice-cool operator displaying bravery well beyond the average as seen in the award of the Silver Cross of Rhodesia (UK equivalent of the DSO) early in his career. As I have mentioned, he certainly impressed me as the K-car commander when we attacked ZANLA at Madulo Pan earlier in the year.

Nick had told him to look me up and we soon struck up a friendship, with us as a family informally adopting him while serving in a strange country. Not that Mike needed any form of cossetting; he was a singular and independent person in his own right. Nevertheless, he spent many of his days off lounging by our pool and many an evening with our friends and us, his. At about this time his three year contract with the Rhodesian Air Force came to an end and to everyone's surprise and disappointment the RhAF declined to renew his contract. We may never know the exact reasons, but contributory to the decision could have been the reality that the procurement of French-built Alouette helicopters in sanctions-burdened Rhodesia was not only difficult but extremely expensive. Since Mike had destroyed at least three of these valuable machines during his heroic escapades, they might have decided that no matter how good and brave an operator he was, they could not risk or afford the loss of any more priceless choppers.

Another factor may have been that although Mike was deeply respectful and loyal to his colleagues fighting on the frontline, his disdain for our leaders, which included most of those ranked above squadron leader or major, was obvious to all.

He checked out of the officers' mess at New Sarum and parked most of his belongings, included his cars and his lovely big, shaggy-haired English sheepdog, Doris, with us for safe keeping. After a brief spell for R&R, he surprised us with the news that he was joining the Selous Scouts, with a promotion to major. Soon after, he took me into his confidence. He revealed that the scouts were sending him on a covert reconnaissance mission to Zambia that would lead to ZAPU leader, Joshua Nkomo's assassination, a prior attempt having failed. He melted out of sight and touch, but soon I was on standby to fly the para-born scouts into Lusaka to accomplish the mission. I went on standby twice at Andre Rabie barracks, the dedicated scouts airfield, but both times we were stood down. There was always a glitch; either the rains had washed away roads or Nkomo, who was constantly on the move fearing threats on his life, was no longer in residence at Freedom House, his personal dwelling in Lusaka.

All went quiet for a time until we heard that he had been captured and was incarcerated in Lusaka prison. I received a letter he had smuggled out of the jail, which more than anything, was a series of coded messages to the scout leadership as to his exact location in the jail, and his condition.

With some difficulty I managed to make an appointment to see Colonel Ron Reid Daly, the founder of the Selous Scouts. I had heard so much about this great leader and military visionary. To say that I came away unimpressed is an understatement. While admitting that the scouts had sent him on the mission, and sympathetic to Mike's

HEADWIND: AN AFRICAN AIR ODYSSEY

plight, he gave me the impression that Borlace's capture and imprisonment was largely of his own making. When I reminded him of the scouts' vow to look after their own at all times, he came across to me as indifferent. By this time Rhodesia was soon to become Zimbabwe and he said there was nothing further he was prepared to do to effect his rescue.

The SAS inherited the task of killing Nkomo, mounting a motorised raid into Lusaka where they successfully reduced Freedom House to rubble. Nkomo was not among the dead, having fled as a result of a tip off, possibly from a pro-Mugabe British mole. The Rhodesian authorities also turned down a request for a side operation to rescue Borelace. Not long after, a photograph of Mike in shackles under escort to a Lusaka court hearing appeared on the front page of our Rhodesian national newspaper, The Herald, which confirmed the rumour of his capture that had been circulating for months. I was able to maintain some contact with him by forwarding letters from his mother and then sending on the occasional message that was smuggled back. By now, Rhodesia had become independent Zimbabwe, with Joshua Nkomo part of the black majority government and Mike Borlace an all but forgotten cause.

Naturally, pilots and soldiers who knew and had operated with Borlace were unhappy but any approach to the military hierarchy to mount a rescue was refused. Jerry Lynch, me, and a few close friends got together to initiate a liberation plan. In simple terms, it involved a sympathetic K-car commander arranging a posting to Kariba where he and his technician/gunner, who was also onside with the scheme, would, early in the morning of the appointed day, arrange a fictitious air task, fly to the Lusaka prison, hover over the exercise yard, and with the 20mm canon, discourage guards' or soldiers' objections. Borelace would somehow make his way to the exercise yard for an uplift. The chopper would then fly to the Rhodesian edge of Lake Kariba, close to one of the airstrips, where a private light aircraft would be waiting to fly him, the K-car pilot and his technician to

South Africa after the pilot had disposed of the chopper into the lake with a boat on hand to pull him out. Ditching the helicopter in the lake would put pursuers and investigators off the scent and make it that much more difficult to determine where the escapee and his accomplices had gone.

The planning of the rescue mission took time. We had to ensure the right people were involved and that they were prepared to abandon their homeland once the mission was accomplished. Eventually, the preparations were complete, and we were ready to go when we heard that inexplicably, the Zambians had released Borelace from prison and deported him back to England. As I say, the rest is his story to tell.

Around the same time, an article appeared in the British *Sunday Times* claiming it had exposed the sanctions-busting operations of Affretair/Air Gabon Cargo, with the result that the British Government had passed a list to the United Nations sanctions committee of Affretair employees, among them Captain Charles Goosens, former French Air Force pilot who was, until a year ago, responsible for flying French President Valéry Giscard d'Estaing's official plane. Whitehall was also withdrawing passport facilities from UK citizens working for the company. The list included Colin Miller, Gus Tattersall, George Dyer, Roger Brackley, Clem Clements, John Fleming, Eddie Morrist, and Phil Palmer, who actually worked for the Rhodesian Department of Civil Aviation and was not employed by Affretair (Air Gabon Cargo).

Many had flown for the Royal Air Force either during World War Two or soon afterwards. My name was absent from list, immediately prompting me to task my mother with obtaining my maternal grandmother's Irish birth certificate. It would allow me to apply for an Irish passport, which I successfully accomplished. Thank you, Ireland.

CHAPTER 15

Crescendo of war—1979

January

The year began in customary form with a trip through the Seychelles to Sharjah, a night stop, on to Muscat, and then straight back to Salisbury.

Both air force and civilian aircraft had been shot down and crew and passengers killed or seriously injured over the past year. The military command decided that it made sense for as many air crew as possible to have the experience of a parachute jump. None of us were particularly excited at the prospect of jumping out of a perfectly serviceable aircraft.

The day after my return from Muscat, I found myself in the Para Training School with a number of other pilots learning the basics of how to parachute. While we were rolling around on the matting and jumping from the gantry in the roof, I learned I had been awarded the Military Forces Commendation (Operational) Medal. The citation reads: 'To denote an act of bravery, distinguished service, or continuous devotion to duty in the operational sphere.'

It was a great honour, but also a humbling reminder of so many other braver service men and women and civilians who had made the ultimate sacrifice, or had their lives changed for ever.

The next day we were all kitted up with our parachutes and herded into the back of a Dakota which flew us over Lake McIlwaine, near Salisbury. Our instructors sensibly chose a water rather than a solid earth landing, to minimise the risk of injury. I felt excited and nervous at the same time.

True to procedure, the red warning light came on and we shuffled towards the open doorway. With the green light we ran in file and leapt out of the aircraft. We were attached to a static line which deployed our parachutes automatically, and after the whirlwind exit, we were soon calmly—almost serenely—drifting lake-wards under billowing canopies of silk into the water below. While we had, without exception, enjoyed the experience, I couldn't help but reflect on how different it must be for troopies to be dropped on their first operational jump into combat. Once fished out of the water, we agreed it was exhilarating and great fun. Our families had driven out to the lake and we all enjoyed a *braai* and lots of beers together.

John Fairey, of the famous Fairey aircraft manufacturing business in the UK, was a captain with British European Airways and then British Airways for many years. He believed Rhodesia was not getting a fair deal, resigned from BA, and joined the RhAF on 3 Squadron flying the DC-3 which he had flown in a previous life. He flew with me to Waterkloof in the middle of the month on an arms run, followed by a trip the next day to Thornhill. He was a charming and thoroughly likeable man.

The following week I did a series of checks to qualify for my Category A command (RhAF) which began with an instrument rating test for my Master Green rating, a necessary requirement for the position. The instrumentation in the DC-3 was very basic with a simple artificial horizon (AH), an airspeed indicator (ASI), an attitude direction indicator (ADI, or more sophisticated form of compass), an altimeter, a turn and slip indicator, a rate of climb and descent indicator (a precursor to the vertical speed indicator or VSI) and a simple magnetic compass. To qualify for the Master Green rating, you had to complete the normal exercises such as rate one turns, steep turns, and unusual attitudes, but on this occasion the ADI, AH, and RCDI were all masked. To make life even harder you had to complete an automatic direction finder (ADF) let down to minima with an overshoot all on one engine with the other having been shut down, and all on a limited instrument panel. Twenty four hours later, I completed the day-into-night check and was able to celebrate the successful check in the mess afterwards.

Right at the end of the month I flew to Bologna with Horse Sweeney where we stayed for a whole week into February, kicking our heels before operating to Ndjamena (Chad), Malta, Bologna, Milan, and Amsterdam before returning home.

February

February proved a bitter-sweet month. It was a doubly bitter time for the nation when on February 12 ZIPRA forces, again using a shoulder-mounted SAM-7 ground to air missile, shot down a second Air Rhodesia civilian Viscount aircraft. Following the deadly route of the first Viscount from Kariba to Salisbury six months earlier, the attack killed all 59 passengers and crew. The world was once again largely silent.

Trying to put this trauma behind me, I dreamed that if I achieved a command of a four-engine jet by the time I was 30 I would have in some way vindicated or put to rest the disastrous start to my aviation career in the RAF. The dream was fulfilled on February 9 when Eddie Morrist passed me on a command check to Brazzaville and back.

Remarkably, of the first four round trips I flew as a captain on the DC-8, each of the first officers with whom I operated all became senior captains with Cathay Pacific after leaving Affretair: Brian Meikle, Richard Hayes, Paddy Hirst, and Tony Norton.

On my third flight as a captain, Paddy Hirst was my flight officer and we flew from Salisbury to Mvengue in Gabon and from there to

Kinshasa before returning. The rain at Kinshasa was torrential when we took off. As we raised the undercarriage, or gear, we felt a tremendous bang and thump. I thought for an instant that we had scraped a hill or even clipped another aircraft, but the plane kept flying and the vibration eventually died down. However, we observed a red warning light indicating a problem: our starboard gear had not locked up. The emergency procedure directed us to reduce speed and re-attempt raising and locking the gear. The red light persisted and only after what felt like an aeon we were relieved to get the green light indicating that all three sets of wheels—nose, port, and starboard bogies—were down and locked.

We decided to stop the procedure there and then; at least we had three sets of wheels locked down, meaning we could land successfully. To add to the drama, our flight engineer, Ken De Goveia, informed us we had lost most of our hydraulic fluid, but he had managed to stop a further leak, though with an absolute minimum of fluid in the reservoir. The flight controls of the DC-8 are mechanical but use hydraulic pressure to assist ease of manual manipulation. You also need hydraulic pressure to adjust the flaps, apply the brakes, and perform a host of other major functions.

Normal emergency procedure required that we land at the nearest suitable airport. Kinshasa was now in a thunderstorm and anyway was politically a non-viable option. Normally, the authorities paid no attention to you as crew operating in and straight out of the airport. However, if you had to night stop, immigration procedures had to be gone through which would prove difficult and embarrassing. We calculated we had enough fuel to limp back to our base which also offered the best prospects of reliable repair. With little hydraulic fluid we could not engage the autopilot, so we had to take turns to manually fly the aircraft, a tough task with the now stiff and heavy flight controls.

With all the gear down, we were restricted to a much lower speed than normal and a maximum altitude of just over 20,000 feet. Under standard conditions, we would have cruised back at around 37,000 feet in about three and a half hours. Flying at the lower altitude and speed, we consumed more fuel than normal. Detouring around several thunderstorms added to our difficulties. However, De Goveia kept a log going, determining that we would make Salisbury with just enough fuel to land but not to divert or miss an approach. It would have to be a text book touch down.

The flight took us just over five hours and when we listened to the landing weather 'actual', we were amused to hear that runway 24 was in use. Ninety nine times out of a hundred, runway 06 is the primary runway at Salisbury because the prevailing wind is normally from the north east. Even if it blows from the south west it is normally light enough to still accommodate a slight tail wind while still using RW 06. That day the wind speed was over 15 knots which meant we had no option but to land on runway 24. It would not have been an issue normally, but 24 did not have an instrument landing system (ILS, a precision navigation and touch down aid) which would have helped us considerably with an accurate approach. Runway 24 is also downhill with a noticeable slope. With reduced hydraulic fluid, we could achieve only 10 degrees of flap, which is used more for take-off than landing. At that setting you produce more lift than drag, resulting in a much higher than normal approach speed.

Salisbury emergency services were alerted and standing by, but the landing and subsequent rollout with no brakes were fortunately uneventful. We taxied off at the end of the runway and our company tug came and towed us back to the apron. It was still early in the morning. Boss Jack, who had been following the drama, came out of his office next to our parking apron to say 'Thanks and well done.'

The Douglas Aircraft Company became involved in the investigation. They established that in the history of the DC-8's operations a similar incident had occurred just three times.

When crew select the undercarriage up command, it triggers the opening of a large, external door. The sequencing valve first programs the retraction arm to pull the wheel bogie into the wheel bay for a hydraulic lock-up. The door is then programmed to close, providing a smooth, drag-free fuselage. What happened in our case? Inexplicably, the sequencing valve malfunctioned. The wheel bay door tried to open at the same time as the retraction arm attempted to haul the landing gear in. The immense counteractive strain sheared a 75 millimetre thick bolt. The door fell back and the retraction arm, now untethered, flailed into the wheel well bay, severing all the main hydraulic lines. Luckily, the offending gear slowly extended due to gravity and clicked into position, so we had all three bogies down and locked, which meant we could at least make a safe landing.

At the time, Affretair held the record for daily operation of the DC-8, and could demonstrate a maintenance record second to none. Neither we as crew nor the airline could be faulted for procedure. I believe Douglas picked up the tab for the repair.

March

March was another busy month with just under 100 hours flown on what were routine flights with both organisations. By now George Alexander had completed his career with the RhAF and had joined Affretair as a first officer on the DC-8. It was a pleasure to be able to fly with him on a couple of occasions to Libreville and back.

April

The political situation was changing rapidly. An election took place involving the entire population. Bishop Abel Muzorewa's United African National Council (UANC) won the majority of seats, but the Rhodesian Front under Ian Smith also secured a considerable number. Joshua Nkomo and Robert Mugabe, who headed the black nationalist Patriotic Front, boycotted the election. The result was a multi-tribal and multi-racial government with Muzorewa as prime minister. The new government of Zimbabwe Rhodesia, as it was now known, went unrecognised by the Patriotic Front, any of the major world powers, or the OAU. Sanctions remained, the ceasefire was broken, and the war continued unabated.

In my view, white Rhodesians historically held a greater respect for the Matabele tribe than for the (Ma)Shona. Joshua Nkomo was the head of ZAPU/ZIPRA, the Matabele faction of the Patriotic Front, while Mugabe led ZANU/ZANLA, dominated by the Shona people. In 1978, Ian Smith met with Nkomo in Lusaka and both signed a deal agreeing they could work together in the future, but the shooting down of the Rhodesian civilian Viscount in September fractured that temporary trust.

The British ominously and disingenuously sided with Mugabe and politicians such as David Owen and Lord Carrington were active in their attempts to destabilise any positive relationship the Rhodesians had with Nkomo. The British had sources at work within the country and when an attempt was about to be made on Mugabe's life he was always tipped off beforehand. An improbable conspiracy theory has circulated that it was the British who were responsible for the destruction of the two Viscounts, purely to discredit Nkomo, although the ZAPU leader brashly and publicly claimed responsibility for their annihilation.

I found it incongruous that this small nation, which had come to Britain's aid during the Second World War to a per capita extent greater than any other country of the empire, including England itself, now found Britain in an alliance with its then current enemies the Soviet Union and China. It seemed incredible that it should wish to bring down subjects who had shown more alliance and allegiance to the crown than any others, and to impose on them a declared Marxist intent on destroying the fabric of one of Britain's once-favourite African assets. We could only surmise—correctly—that they [Britain] were intent on installing a violent, tribalistic, and paranoid monster. His barbaric reign would murder scores of thousands of innocent people and devastate a beautiful, prosperous country in the process. Britain has much to reflect on, and perhaps to answer for.

Later in the month I completed what was to be my last bush tour at

Grand Reef which involved mostly resupply operations across the border. Affretair also afforded me a fascinating sortie into Algiers.

May to August

The period involved a few military missions, but most of the flying operations to new destinations were on the DC-8. Always watchful of detection under sanctions, we had shifted our centre of operations in Holland to Maastricht from which we would fly to Larnaca (Cyprus), Khartoum (Sudan), Mombasa, Barcelona, and Sharjah apart from our normal destinations in Africa.

The fuel crisis of that era affected the availability of aviation fuel throughout our network, so we would tanker fuel whenever we could. At the beginning of June, we were due to fly from Maastricht to Libreville, but in the early stages of our flight we had to shut down one of the engines. Modern practice would have you land at the nearest suitable airport, but we knew a spare engine was available at our base, and having enough fuel on board, I elected, with the concurrence of the rest of the crew, to fly home. We also knew we had suitable alternative airports along our route should a further emergency arise. Eleven and a half hours after departing we arrived, unscheduled, at Salisbury. Once again, Boss Jack came out to thank us; we had saved the company a vast sum of money and kept our operation alive to fight another round.

In July I had orders to return a South African Air Force Dakota to a military base at Pietersburg where it would undergo routine maintenance, and bring another aircraft back. I was pleased but humbled to have as my co-pilot the legendary Captain Chum Keyter former World War Two and Korean War veteran, now flying with Air Rhodesia but also performing a stint on 3 Squadron. We spent an enjoyable six sectors together during our journey south.

September

Rhodesia's Combined Operations decided to exert more pressure on President Kaunda of Zambia and thus Nkomo by cutting the major supply line for Zambia from Tanzania provided by the TAZARA (TanZam) rail link between Lusaka and the port of Dar es Salaam. The rail link was Zambia's lifeline to the port, bringing in thousands of tons of life-sustaining cargo a month. The railway crossed a giant rail bridge over the Chambeshi River in the north east of the country. About 600 meters away a large road bridge would also need to be put out of action. The logistics of mounting an attack against the bridgeheads was significant, with distance the major factor. The bridges were nearly 500 miles from Salisbury and almost 200 from the Rhodesian border. The plan was to drop a four man SAS free fall parachute team in the vicinity of the bridges. They would exit the aircraft following their container carrying explosives, weapons, radios, and supplies under a parachute which would open using a barometric delay device. They would free fall formatting on the box which had a light attached. When they saw its parachute deploy they would pull their ripcords and follow it to earth. Once established on the ground they would walk and paddle canoes, stored in the container, to navigate the river to the bridges, where they would make a full reconnaissance. Having determined the viability of the mission, another team of 12 SAS paratroops would drop in with more explosives and equipment to complete the operation.

The DC-7 was chosen as the delivery aircraft. Captain Jack flew several exploratory missions, not only to find a suitable drop zone away from habitation and thick vegetation, but also to rehearse several parachute free fall missions using a dam close to Salisbury.

Coinciding with a favourable moon, the mission was scheduled for the night of September 12. I was chosen as third pilot on the mission, with Captain Jack, George Alexander, and Flight Engineer John Hodges. My main function was to liaise between the cockpit and the SAS team in the back as the only intercom was between the dispatchers and the cockpit. Leading the SAS team was my friend and colleague, Major Grahame Wilson. We climbed to 13,000 feet and set course, initially across Mozambique and the Cabora Bassa lake before turning north over Zambia. I went back regularly to check on Grahame and his team who were huddled in blankets against the cold. As he was shivering so much I asked if we should turn up the heating, only to receive the reply that the shaking was pure fear and no amount of heat would relieve it.

Once over the target area we could not see the ground through a thick haze prevalent at that time of year, and trapped under an unexpected high pressure system. To avoid any compromise, we knew we could not circle for any length of time, so the mission was aborted. We now had to wait for the next favourable moon phase in a few weeks' time. On the night of September 29, I was again part of the same crew when we dropped Grahame and his free fallers on a final practice jump near Darwendale dam. Operation Cheese, as it was now named, would take place during the next full moon.

Meanwhile, we continued to lose aircraft to enemy fire. The military hierarchy felt that as many aircrew as possible should learn some survival skills in case they were shot down and had to find their way to safety. Six of us from 3 Squadron were flown to a desolate area adjacent to Kariba dam where the Selous Scouts had set up a survival and tracking school. With characteristic grim humour, they named the location Wafa Wafa, loosely translated locally as 'If you die, you die' or "I am dead ... I am dead'. Here, their top instructors taught survival techniques as well as basic and advanced tracking skills. Some of the black soldiers who completed the advanced course became so adept they could track terrorists from an airborne heli-copter. We spent five days living rough in the bush, eating whatever we could forage during the day while learning bush survival methods. Roots, grubs, worms, and leaves became our daily diet, supplemented once with raw liver from a small buck we shot. Our instructors even encouraged us to eat a dead baboon's head which we cooked under the fire at the centre of our camping area. None of us were quite hungry enough to take up the offer, and I was able to describe the location of our meal to a tracker who had just finished his course and hadn't eaten for three days. Our head mysteriously disappeared overnight, much to our relief. Our scout instructors treated us with scant regard though their skills and teaching were excellent. It was one of the best courses I have ever attended, appealing warmly to my inner African.

We were taught how to track and anti-track. On the final day, just after first light, we were dropped off in the middle of the bush miles from camp and given a 20 minute start before the recent advanced training course graduates set off after us. Our task was to avoid capture and return to camp before dark. Wafa Wafa was also located in a remote area where all species of African wildlife roamed freely. At one point, we found ourselves in the middle of a herd of elephants when we decided to use the long grass to cover our tracks. In case we ran into terrorists we had two magazines each for our FN rifles, plus a live round up the spout, ready for immediate use. We ran for the first 20 minutes up into a rocky, hilly area and then anti-tracked for some time before setting off for the nearby lake shore. We calculated it would be more difficult to track us if part of our travels took us through water, crocodiles notwithstanding. As luck would have it, we spotted a boat occupied by two white farmers on a fishing expedition. They were more than happy to ferry us across the bay and drop us on the far side of the camp. We lay up for the rest of the day and strolled in to camp just before dark, much to the amazement of the instructors and trackers. They applauded our skill in avoiding capture, and we were canny enough not to admit to the truth of our success, rationalising to ourselves that the means justified the end in war.

October

Finally, on the night of October 3, conditions smiled favourably on Operation Cheese and Grahame Wilson and his team free fell out of the DC-7 deep into Zambia. By October 16, the SAS had demolished the two bridges over the Chambeshi River severing the link between Zambia and Tanzania, a considerable and strategic coup. Kaunda was beside himself with rage and frustration, insisting Nkomo come to some agreement with the Rhodesian regime.

Meanwhile, ComOps had received intelligence that ZIPRA was planning a conventional cross border invasion of Rhodesia with a plan to capture major towns close to the border and then on to seize Salisbury. They would use considerable infantry forces accompanied by masses of armoured vehicles. Libyan aircraft would provide support and transport, and Soviet MiG jets would offer air cover. To counteract this threat, ComOps elected to destroy as many bridges in Zambia as necessary making it impossible for an armoured column to travel across Zambia and over the Rhodesian border. Over the next few weeks, the SAS destroyed a further seven bridges, disrupting vital links to the south east and south west of Zambia, and strangling ZIPRA's ability to manoeuvre along those routes.

Politically, the leading western powers and the United Nations exerted more and more pressure on all fronts to force the Rhodesians to commit to elections that represented all parties, including ZANLA and ZIPRA. Neither had taken part in the previous election that installed Bishop Abel Muzorewa as prime minister. For such an election to take place, an overall ceasefire was necessary and indemnities would need to be extended to all terrorists who would have to be in the country to vote. It was an unpalatable solution for the Rhodesians, but the international pressure was by now extreme. A pivotal conference involving all parties was about to commence in London at Lancaster House.

In the meantime, the Rhodesian security forces were fully occupied trying to contain intensified hostilities as well as confronting increasing numbers of terrorists gathering in Zambia and Mozambique. They were desperate to return to Rhodesia to cause as much damage and unrest as they could in order to expedite an agreement.

Late in the month I received orders from 3 Squadron to fly down to

Swartkop, a South African military base just south of Pretoria, and from there to Durban for a night and day stop before making our return journey via Swartkop and our main air force base at Thornhill. It brought about a pleasant break and a welcome load of weapons on our return. The South Africans had become much more supportive under their new president, P.W. Botha. They could see what Britain was trying to do to Rhodesia, with whom they had considerable sympathy. The South African foreign minister, Pik Botha, said, 'the Zimbabwe Rhodesia settlement issue is beginning to look like a rugby match where the game is played until the winners lose'. White Rhodesians shared these sentiments as the British now prepared to draw up a new constitution and to supervise new elections involving all parties, Mugabe's and Nkomo's factions included. Rhodesians saw it as an unwinnable situation.

As busy as ever with Affretair, I flew to Libreville, Abidjan, Tunis, Larnaca, Khartoum, Mombasa, Amsterdam, and Johannesburg during the month.

November

With the capitulation of the Portuguese in Mozambique to FRELIMO, the new president of Mozambique, Samora Machel, had introduced severe measures that immediately upset a great proportion of the population. Disgruntled Mozambicans quickly formed an armed opposition group called the Mozambique Resistance Movement (MNR), whose sole purpose was to overthrow FRELIMO. This suited the Rhodesians well and soon the SAS and the MNR were working together targeting installations around the country. They set up their headquarters in the thick bush area of the Serra de Gorongoza mountains of Sofala province. HQ was a mountain rising to an altitude of 6,100 feet above the surrounding lowlands with a flat top of meadows and streams surrounded by protective forests which made concealment ideal.

Part of our regular routine during this period was to fly resupply missions, code named Operation Bumper, to the hilltop where we would drop supplies or sometimes troops by parachute. We found these trips mostly enjoyable because the anti-aircraft factor was reduced to almost zero. The MNR personnel who ran out to greet the arrival of new supplies would form a huge crowd of at times thousands, all waving cheerfully. It was a relief to see so many combatants without weapons pointing our way.

However, in the lowlands of Mozambique, the SAS were still at work and needed regular resupplies. On one afternoon sortie, I was the leader in a two-ship formation, flying much-needed supplies to an SAS contingent over the border. The plan was that approaching the drop zone my number two would fall back and the SAS would talk me in for the despatch, repeating the process for my deputy. As we had more than two drop loads aboard, I would perform a gentle orbit and reposition for the next drop with my number two following behind as before. To keep radio telephony transmissions to a minimum the SAS commander was only communicating with me but his instructions for red light on, and then green light on were repeated for the second aircraft. Unfortunately, as I was approaching for my second drop the dispatchers in the second aircraft did not realise the first set of instructions were for my dispatchers, and theirs would follow next. Apparently, on hearing the green light command, they bundled out their cargo, sadly far removed from the drop zone. The consignment disappeared into thick bush, never to be retrieved by the apoplectic SAS. As the story goes, Captain Darryl Watt, the SAS commander, is still looking for Whiskey Three (me) and when he finds him, he'll kill him!

John Fairey's despatcher in the second Dak made the error, but as I was the lead aircraft, the SAS troops on the ground understandably knew no better than to blame me. I look on it as my only blemish in delivering to the SAS.

On November 25 I did another clandestine trip with Captain Jack and John Hodges as the flight engineer from Salisbury to Comoros and from there to Waterkloof, the military base in South Africa before returning to Salisbury with a plane load of arms and munitions.

December

The beginning of the month saw an operation northbound in the DC-8 to Libreville, Tunis, and Amsterdam before returning via Libreville and Kinshasa. On December 7, I had the pleasure of flying an Operation Bumper resupply with our new squadron commander, Tudor Thomas, who was just converting onto the Dakota.

Four days later, having borrowed my father's truck, we loaded the children, and Doris, Mike Borelace's dog, into the back, and drove to Beatrice, a village 35 miles south west of Salisbury. There, at 0730, we lined up in the convoy for our road trip to Natal to begin. At this point in the war, driving alone any distance beyond the main cities was not only dangerous but forbidden. The possibility of a terrorist ambush was high, and many had taken place.

The army established a daily convoy system where a couple of armoured vehicles would escort any vehicles who wished to drive to South Africa from Salisbury. Once all the cars had assembled at 0730, one armoured car would take the lead and the other would follow behind with all the civilian vehicles in the middle. To minimise the chances of an ambush, the convoy travelled at a set speed of 60 to 65 miles an hour. Some underpowered cars would struggle to keep up and the length of the convoy would steadily increase. We would take two refreshment, petrol, and toilet stops en route to Beit Bridge (the border between Rhodesia and South Africa) during the 180-mile journey. Safely at the border, the armoured vehicles would farewell us before turning around and escorting another convoy of vehicles making their way north to Salisbury.

The past year had been a great strain on everyone. It was time for a well-earned holiday on the coast of Natal with our close friends, David and Sarie Pithey.

The Lancaster House talks dragged on for months but finally drew to an end with the signing of an agreement on December 21 while we enjoyed the sea and the sun. The basics of the agreement were far-reaching. It nullified the declaration of independence of 1965. It dissolved Zimbabwe-Rhodesia as a state. Britain re-assumed rule prior to another election. It declared a cease fire which in effect ended the war. The agreement extended an amnesty to all ZANU and ZAPU guerrillas, who would also be eligible to stand for election. Finally, it lifted sanctions against Rhodesia, or Southern Rhodesia as it was once again called.

We enjoyed a stress-free Christmas before driving home without the need of the convoy from Beit Bridge. We made the most of the New Year celebrations, sharing the occasion with colleagues who had been stuck in the bush for years. However, despite the cessation of hostilities, an ominous, and sometimes overwhelming dread of the future prevailed.

So ended the last year of Rhodesia as we knew it. Many feared what lay ahead, but nothing we projected then could approach the evil that followed.

CHAPTER 16

Bicycle rescues jet airliner—gun-running in Africa—1980

January

The atmosphere in Salisbury was strange. Hostilities had ceased. A British governor ruled the country, and a steady stream of Commonwealth observers to monitor the forthcoming elections flowed into the country courtesy of the Royal Air Force. Many welcomed the British, housing and entertaining them. Some of my ex-Cranwell friends flew into New Sarum and took up accommodation at the officers' mess.

After all I had gone through, I struggled to come terms with what felt like another invasion. I found it all but impossible to embrace anybody from Britain involved in the transition. I saw them, even unwittingly, as part of the agony of having us hand over our country to those intent on killing us and thousands of their own innocent people, and destroying a prosperous country through mass violence rather than sustained negotiation. Of course we were accused of the same bias. War cares little for distinctions between history, truth, and justice.

But I felt dreadfully betrayed.

Rather than suffocate in this surreal atmosphere, we flew as a family to Europe in the back of the DC-8, to catch up with Jennifer's sister and brother-in-law stationed in Germany. We then joined up with Sam Richman and his family for a two week skiing holiday in the small resort of Alpbach in Austria, an exotic and refreshing distraction after the turbulence of recent months. We returned to Salisbury in the back of the DC-8, a spell-binding experience for the children since we were the only passengers. With none of the strictures of contemporary aviation, they could wander freely through the fuselage, and make tea in the galley for us and the crew.

Back at work I first completed all my recency requirements to requalify with 3 Squadron. It remained active, resupplying the still-manned FAFs, and supporting the parachute training school to keep all paratroops trained and current. Although the war was officially over, Operation Bumper went on with elements of the SAS still based in Mozambique and the MNR needing regular resupply. Operations like these continued covertly in the background without the British governing authorities needing (or perhaps even wanting) to know.

I could also return to normal flying on the DC-8. Now that sanctions had been lifted, Affretair operated unfettered as a charter cargo airline with our main loads still beef out of Salisbury and our code share operation from Amsterdam to Johannesburg once a week. Instead of secrecy and subterfuge, we could operate legally to all our regular ports and no longer had overflight issues en route to our many destinations. It made February a demanding month with the normal ratio of 3 Squadron duties combined with Affretair excursions to Tunis, Amsterdam, Libreville, Brazzaville, and Johannesburg.

March

Was this our darkest hour? Supposed free and fair elections took place throughout the country. However, clear evidence of ZANU and ZAPU intimidation emerged under the noses of purportedly neutral UN observers and Commonwealth monitoring forces. It went unheeded, or, if heeded, unpunished. Consequently, the result so many dreaded was announced on March 4 1980: Robert Mugabe's ZANU party had convincingly won the election, making Mugabe our new prime minister. He immediately changed the name of the country to Zimbabwe. Words can barely describe my feelings of disbelief and despair. A poor analogy I suppose would be how the population of Great Britain may have felt if the Germans had invaded in 1940 and established a German government. I had vowed some time back that if Mugabe did gain power by whatever means, I would leave my country. I now had to put my words into practice.

Some members of our armed forces, thoroughly disillusioned with the current state of affairs, had left Rhodesia and were helping the Republic of Transkei, a nominally independent homeland within South Africa, establish an efficient and stable defence force. I am sure the British during the transition period were unaware of our assisting former security force personnel such as Selous Scouts founder, Ron Reid Daly and company, who had based themselves in the capital, Umtata (now Mthatha).

Soon after the election I was tasked to take a plane load of ordnance and munitions down to Transkei. We flew from Salisbury to Swartkop to collect additional equipment and from there to Durban to refuel before setting course to Umtata which is slightly inland from the coast. Without facilities there to accommodate us we quickly unloaded and returned to Durban. On the way down from Durban we had flown the standard designated air routes, but for the return journey we requested and received clearance for a low level visual flight rules (VFR). We headed straight for the coast before turning north, flying at just a couple of hundred feet above the sea and adjacent to some of the most beautiful and rugged coastline you could imagine. It is not called the Wild Coast by accident. At times we flew below the clifftops from which tumbled awe inspiring waterfalls. It has imprinted itself on my mind as one of the most memorable sectors of my flying career.

Later in the month I completed a long Affretair pattern flying to Brazzaville, Libreville, Las Palmas, Amsterdam, Cairo, Sanaa (Yemen), Tunis, and Johannesburg. It meant I was still working well over the monthly limit of 60 flying hours, but that was of no great concern since we were still operating on our Gabonese and Omani licenses; neither aircraft was yet re-registered in Zimbabwe.

April

Even in these unsettled times, a thinly gratifying sense of civility prevailed. Malloch and John Fairey hosted social occasions on consecutive evenings, noting our contribution to a troubled history. In the light of these events, Fairey decided that his service to 3 Squadron was no longer relevant and he would return to the UK. Mournfully, he died in a light aircraft accident in his homeland a few years later.

On April 18, Rhodesia formally became independent Zimbabwe with Mugabe as prime minister. Ian Smith's often-misquoted dream of 1,000 years of white rule had come to an end in a little more than a dozen after UDI.

When I first joined Air Trans Africa our operations manager was a delightful World War Two veteran, Group Captain Jack Blanchard-Simms, with Captain Colin Miller as chief pilot. It was a strong management team for the most part, and one that kept us happy. With the changing political scene and for personal reasons, both resigned at much the same time and George Dyer took over as the operations manager with John Webb assuming chief pilot duties. They faced great difficulties given the turbulence of the era and two sometimes irreconcilably different characters. Our two training captains, Eddie Morrist and 'Clem' Clements, both very experienced, soon clashed with George, and to try to resolve the situation they both resigned, thinking that George would capitulate because the airline would no longer have the examiners necessary to keep us legal. This posed no problem to George who promptly offered me and Sam Richman promotion to training captain, which we both accepted.

Until then both of us enjoyed a good working relationship with Eddie and Clem based on our respect for their seniority and experience compared to ours. Our elevation, though perfectly legitimate, now caused friction between me and Eddie, a tension which never really reached a resolution. However, after a time I received a delightful letter from Clem congratulating me, praising my approach, and offering his assistance should I ever need it.

In the middle of the month we positioned to the KLM simulator in Amsterdam to master both the fixed base and moving simulators, in due course qualifying as approved operators. Phil Palmer from the now Zimbabwean DCA examined and passed us both as approved examiners on the DC-8 simulator. I flew back with Phil to Harare via Tunis, Libreville, and Johannesburg, operating from both seats which qualified me as a DC-8 instrument and type rating examiner, a huge step in my aviation career. The company sent details to both the Gabonese and Omani DCAs and I soon received certificates approving me as a DC-8 examiner approved by their authorities.

May

The ink on my examiner license barely dry, management called me to the airport to perform an instrument rating check on Boss Jack. His license and rating were about to expire. I dreaded the challenge. Having flown extensively with Jack I knew instrument flying was not something he enjoyed or excelled at.

The check did not go as well as I would have hoped. The first approach was out of limits and I had to instruct Boss Jack to repeat it. In the process I explained that his use of the rudder was insufficient to counter the asymmetry caused by shutting down one engine.

I recall two touching moments after the check was complete and we landed. First, after the debrief, Captain Jack apologised for his performance and thanked me for my direction on the use of the rudder. He revealed his instructors at United Airlines in the US had not been as clear or succinct during his conversion course. Second, John Hodges, the senior check engineer said, 'You're a brave man to make the Boss do another approach, but you were right.'

I came to the unvoiced personal conclusion that if the Boss ever needed another check, Sam Richman would have to do it.

3 Squadron flying had dropped off considerably though para dropping details, the odd resupply to the MNR and SAS in Mozambique, and the daily shuttles between the main airfields, which the army and air force still manned, continued.

Late in the month I flew to Amsterdam to successfully conduct my first set of recurrent checks in the simulator.

June

A few air force operations in the middle of the month included flying the new president of Zimbabwe, the Reverend Canaan Banana to Umtali (Mutare) for the day. However, much of the rest of my flying time was devoted to Affretair.

Cargoman was an Omani registered air cargo company with, among other directors, Dr Omar Zawawi, who was the founder and Managing Director, while his brother, Qais Zawawi, also a director, was additionally the Omani foreign minister. In 1979 while Qais was visiting the United Kingdom on official business, he had a meeting with a government representative called Treadwell who awkwardly tried to point out that Cargoman was merely a front for Air Gabon Cargo, the Rhodesian sanctions-busting airline, and that the British Government planned to submit a report as such to the United Nations Sanctions Committee. Zawawi, apparently very non-committal, reminded Treadwell of several agreements signed between the UK and Oman resulting in considerable benefits to

Britain, including the strategically important control of the Straits of Hormuz on behalf of the west.

Britain tendered a half-hearted complaint with the result that Cargoman continued to operate successfully for the next couple of years. Now that Zimbabwe was independent, Tim Landon, a wealthy British adviser to the Omani government, and the Zawawi brothers, were not keen on a close association with the Mugabe regime and its allegiance to Marxism. They tried to persuade Malloch to move the whole operation to Oman, with Muscat as Cargoman's main base. Jack was tempted but for the moment he wished to keep the whole operation in Zimbabwe. The lengthy and costly restoration of his World War Two Spitfire was nearing completion and may have influenced his decision to remain in Zimbabwe.

At the end of June, I flew as Jack's co-pilot to Muscat, with John Hodges as the flight engineer. We arrived in the early hours of the morning and while the aircraft was loaded with a cargo of weapons and military hardware, Jack went off for a meeting with the Zawawi brothers and Landon. We spent little time on the ground before taking off again with Waterkloof as our destination to offload and return to Harare (formerly Salisbury) after more than 20 hours on our mission.

Sadly for me, it was the last time I was to fly with Jack. We joined him in his office for a drink where he announced that, for medical reasons, he could no longer hold a professional pilot's licence but would continue to fly the Spitfire on a private pilot's licence. As he could no longer fly the type of sortie we had just completed, he asked if I would be prepared to continue the smersh, or clandestine missions that would come up from time to time, without him. The reality was we were now aiding the South Africans who were in turn assisting UNITA under Savimbi's command in his attempt to depose the Marxist government then in power. Of course I was honoured, and readily agreed.

It was a telling moment when John Hodges, his faithful comrade and companion in the cockpit for many years, decided Zimbabwe was no longer the country he wished to live in. He, George Dyer, and Chris Higginson, all long serving stalwarts, had recently resigned, a sign that Affretair would never quite be the same again.

July

The month saw several more air force assignments, but again, my time was mostly taken up on Affretair business with a week-long stint in Amsterdam carrying out simulator checks. Late in the month, the Zambian authorities released Mike Borlace from prison in Lusaka, returning him to the UK. His release foiled the highly secret plan in which I was involved with a handful of selected conspirators to effect his liberation, as described in Chapter 14. Once he had caught up with his family and probably undergone a UK Special Branch debrief, he was hoping to return to Zimbabwe to sort out his belongings and see his precious dog, Doris. I spent some time researching if his return might jeopardise his safety, but as the government had granted an amnesty to all combatants, it appeared he was clear to come back. I asked Jack if we could fly him from Europe at some later date in the DC-8 and he readily consented to the flight and a reunion.

August

August was another relatively quiet month with some flying on the Dakota. Late in the month I operated up to Amsterdam and Mike Borlace flew across for a night's stay in the Schiphol Hilton with us before we flew him back to Harare. When we arrived outside our house, Mike merely called 'hey' and in an instant a huge ball of joyous canine fur came hurtling out of the house and down the veranda to greet his grievously missed master. If the possessive pronoun seems odd, it was a touch of Borelace humour; Doris was unquestionably a male. Doris's touching welcome escalated into a night-long celebration for someone approaching a prodigal son.

Adventure in Kamina

September saw an incredibly busy month with more than 110 hours flown, approaching double the regulated limit. On September 11 I received my brief on the first of the smersh trips without Jack or John Hodges, who had left for South Africa. George Alexander was the first officer with Dave Goldsmith the flight engineer and Skitch Roberts the loadmaster. We took off in the evening and flew to Kinshasa in the DRC where we loaded some military hardware before making our way to the Waterkloof military base in South Africa. While they unloaded and reloaded, we snatched a few hours' sleep in a nearby hotel before departing late in the afternoon for a return to Kinshasa.

Kinshasa this time was purely a fuel stop, as our destination was the military air base, Kamina, into which I had previously flown with Jack. Kamina lacked the refuelling facilities to accommodate aircraft the size of our DC-8, only their own smaller military aircraft. For security reasons, and for the secrecy and success of the operation, it was of paramount importance that we arrived in darkness and departed before dawn.

Our arrival into Kamina was uneventful. We were obviously expected. Skitch made sure that the large cargo door was opened prior to us shutting down as there was no ground power unit (GPU) at Kamina compatible with the DC-8. Once we shut the aircraft down we would have no electrical power whatsoever. The welcoming ground troops had a forklift to unload the military gear we had brought in as well as reload some other sensitive ordnance. The weapons and ammunition we had delivered would soon arm Jonas Savimbi's UNITA organisation which was fighting against Angola's ruling MPLA, a left wing client of the Soviet Union and Cuba. At the same time, both the US and South Africa supported UNITA in its stand against a communist regime. As a neighbour to Angola, the DRC had to tread a politically discrete path so as to not incur the wrath of the Soviets or Cubans.

It was crucial for us to arrive and depart under cover of darkness in order to attract minimal attention. The unloading and reloading proceeded according to plan. All we had to do was fire up our portable GPU which we needed to start an engine. Worryingly, several noisy attempts made it obvious that the GPU was not going to start since both igniters needed to initiate the spark for the jet fuel had failed. A single igniter failure happened occasionally, but the failure of both simultaneously was extraordinary. Ground staff should have carried out a functionality check before we left which no doubt would have revealed that one igniter had already failed. The second had decided to quit when we needed it most. We were now grounded with an effectively dead aircraft. Not only were we stranded, we were on the apron of a foreign military air base that, neutral in the dark, would turn distinctly hostile as dawn broke, only a few hours away.

Our power situation was dire. We had so little emergency electrical standby power we could not even use the HF radio. What to do? We had to come up with a plan quickly and it was vital to notify base so they could get the wheels in motion to rescue us, or at least attempt to mitigate our fate. However, I had a germ of an idea as to how we might start the aircraft, but first I needed to contact home. An army garrison guarded the airfield. I was sure its HQ tent in the bush would have radio equipment.

I asked if I could meet the army commander who, like everyone else I spoke to, was courteous and polite rather than hostile. Under the circumstances they had every right to be suspicious considering we were white English-speaking intruders and they were black French-speaking military. He was a young officer and was only too happy to help as best he could. He must have understood that our presence the next day would cause extreme embarrassment and potentially spark an international diplomatic crisis. I asked if I could use their high frequency radio set, which I was sure they possessed because HF was the standard form of medium to long range communication in those days long before the invention of satellite communications. However, their communication was not by HF but by VHF (short range) as they had no real need for long range comms. After much discussion, they unearthed a small back-pack radio. I guessed at and correctly selected the right frequency on the selector panel which we used as our primary frequency with which to communicate with our base call sign, Affro. As it had not been used for a while the battery pack was flat.

As we often say, 'only in Africa', and ingenuity came to the rescue. Our army friends produced a stationary bicycle frame equipped with a small dynamo. With furious pedalling, the radio battery could be re-charged. It was a hot and humid night and the poor soldier tasked with pedalling was soon drenched in sweat. After an anxiety laden interval, the power indicator needle began to climb. I tried calling Affro on both the main frequencies with no response. The poor soldier had to keep up a non-stop effort; each attempted call exhausted the battery. Despairing, I tried our 89 frequency one more time and got a very faint 'go ahead'. I quickly explained our dilemma and requested they contact Mandir, Malloch's code name (we never used actual names on radio transmissions to avoid any possible identification) to initiate a rescue plan.

In the meantime, my germ of an idea on how to solve our problem began to expand like a cell dividing. I explained that we had very limited means of communication and that it was unlikely we would be able to provide regular updates. My message was acknowledged with a final 'good luck' sign off as my colleague on the other end knew it was almost certain we would be arrested and imprisoned sometime the next day for arms trafficking.

Daylight was fast approaching. All the ground staff had disappeared with their equipment, leaving the apron deserted apart from this large jet aircraft with its cargo door open. I reasoned that if my idea was to work, we would have only a narrow window of daylight in which to attempt it, before the eyes of the world, and more specifically the eyes of the DRC's politicians, woke up to our presence. We managed a short nap before dawn which in that part of Africa is very close to six o'clock when most military organisations start their day. In no time, the apron had transformed into a parade ground with the immaculate line-up of hundreds of soldiers staring incredulously at this monstrous beast.

Years before, my brother, Tony, told me an amazing story in which a Boeing 707, caught in a similar situation to ours, had used a Buffalo turbo-prop aircraft to provide propeller wash from its engine to rotate the 707 engine sufficiently to get it started. In simplified form, it is analogous to push-starting a manual car. I hoped to use the same technique using one of the Kamina base fighter or trainer aircraft to do the same for us.

First though, I had to sell the idea to the air force base commander, a very imposing black colonel in full operational regalia. In my stumbling schoolboy French I explained my idea, which he appeared to receive with serious scepticism. I could tell he was also nervous of the consequences if he did not get rid of us as soon as possible. He reluctantly agreed to try.

They opened the hangar doors and wheeled out a smart new-looking Italian-designed Aermacchi MB 326 fighter/trainer aircraft which we carefully positioned in front of our starboard inboard engine. If started successfully, we would use it to cross bleed start our other engines. The colonel announced that as he was the base commander, he would take responsibility and occupy the cockpit of the fighter himself. Since we had no other means of communicating, we agreed a series of hand signals which we would use to exchange directions. I would occupy the right hand cockpit seat of the DC-8 and with my side window open I could look down on him below me in his fighter. We were reasonably confident that we had aligned the exhaust jet pipe of the fighter sufficiently close to our engine intake to give the optimal air flow through our engine rotor blades.

We positioned ourselves in our aircraft and he started his small jet. The noise was considerable but probably no more than that of our

GPU if it were working. He had positioned the biggest chocks he could find in front of each of the fighter's wheels, but they still looked tiny and insignificant from where I was sitting. I also noticed that he had applied the park brake as part of his prestart set up. It took some time for him to signal that the engine warm up time was sufficient for him to open the throttle and increase thrust, of which we would need maximum. The soldiers had now retired from the apron but remained in formation on the airstrip boundary watching in fascination.

Without becoming too technical, to start the Pratt and Whitney JT3D engine fitted to the DC-8 we needed a 12 per cent minimum rotation of the N1 rotor before we could engage the fuel switch which would provide jet fuel and initiate the igniter. We would then have the correct mixture of air and fuel for successful ignition. Once burning, the process would be continuous until the engine was shut down by switching off the fuel. If we initiated the fuel earlier, we ran the risk of what is termed a hot start. This occurs when the fuel ignites in the combustion chamber with insufficient air supplied to allow for full combustion. When the exhaust gas temperatures (EGT) exceed 800C, flames erupt from the back of the engine which must be shut down immediately to prevent catastrophic damage.

The colonel below me in his cockpit had by now selected full thrust. The aircraft, which was pointing directly at the hangar in front of it, began to strain against the chocks. By now his face was glistening and his sky coloured shirt had turned navy blue with sweat. In our cockpit the needle showing our N1 rpm had barely begun to move. A further age passed before the gauge crept away from zero. The colonel fixed me in his gaze, desperate for some sign of progress. All I could do was beg for more time and more thrust from his already quivering fighter jet. At about six per cent rpm, which was too low for fuel initiation, the needle stagnated. I signalled, waving my hand up indicating we needed more at our end. I watched him nervously push the throttle into the emergency power range. By now the noise was deafening and the fighter aircraft was violently bucking against its brakes and chocks like an enraged stallion straining to break free of its tethers. It was obvious to me that the colonel was justifiably terrified. If the fighter jumped the chocks, it would catapult like a bullet straight into the hangar.

Our N1 gauge had dawdled to between seven and eight per cent. Weighing up all the factors as best I could, I decided 'now or never' and slammed the fuel cut off switch to engaged. After a few seconds the N1 gauge began to climb again but the EGT gauge shot up past the red line of maximum allowable temperature. Dave was screaming to cut the fuel, but I blocked his hand. Slowly, magically, the N1 stabilised at the idle rpm and the EGT fell back below its red line. Our engine had started.

I signalled down to the colonel to shut down and he resignedly throttled back to idle and allowed his engine the necessary cool down time. I could see from his body language that he was shattered that our plan had failed. What he didn't know was that the din of his own jet had deafened him to the sound of our engine roaring into life. The look of relief on his face as he shut his engine down and heard the powerful whine of ours behind him gave me an unforgettable picture of joy and amazement.

I instructed, George and Dave to continue with the cross bleed start procedure for the other engines and while Skitch closed the cargo door I ran down the stairs onto the apron having first grabbed as many US$100 dollar bills as I could squeeze into my tightly clenched hand. The colonel was there to meet me. In the emotion of the moment, and our haste to see the back of each other, we had little time for mutual congratulations. We managed to exchange a heart-felt bear hug and a firm but discreet hand-shake for the clandestine currency exchange. With his right hand firmly in his pocket, a now grinning colonel waved us away with his left.

I turned at the top of the stairs, gave him the best salute I could muster, and with that sped to my seat for George to get us aloft, out of danger, and on our way back to Waterkloof.

No sooner had we got airborne than I contacted base to tell them we had escaped successfully. I had also to admit to Jack that in the process we may have cooked one of his engines. Strangely, the courageous number three engine ran perfectly with all temperatures and pressures at normal, so unaffected that our ground maintenance team cleared us to operate to Waterkloof before returning to base.

I am not aware of a similar occasion where the jet efflux of a small fighter helped start a large jet engine. Pratt and Whitney would probably maintain it was impossible. But the four of us in that aircraft and the air base colonel knew that, extraordinarily, it had worked. I still reflect on the adventure and how close we came to execution or lengthy jail sentences for, at best, gun-running, or at worst, involvement in an attempted coup.

We arrived back at base where an extremely grateful Boss met and thanked us, inviting us into his us into his office to recount our adventure over drinks.

A few days later, I flew a meat delivery flight up to Amsterdam and Zurich followed by a return charter from Amsterdam to Kano, Nigeria, before being summoned back to base for another smersh flight. On this occasion George, Dave, and I were part of a dual crew with Colin Miller, to spread the workload since we had a very busy schedule ahead of us. We had to be careful operating directly to a South African military base because politically, Zimbabwe and South Africa were now aligned to virtually opposite loyalties, with Zimbabwe under Mugabe embracing a form of communism. So we started our journey by delivering meat to Libreville before flying to Waterkloof to collect some more military hardware.

South Africa had constructed a large military base at Grootfontein in South West Africa (soon to become Namibia) from which to combat the growing conflict with SWAPO, the militant organisation fighting for the independence of South West Africa. Neighbouring Angola gave them shelter, along with accommodating extensive Cuban and Russian forces. South Africa also gave aid to South West

Africa and to Jonas Savimbi's UNITA rebels fighting to topple the communist regime ruling Angola. For the South African Defence Forces (SADF) it was an asymmetric conflict. They used us to assist with various assignments because we could now fly throughout Africa unhindered. UNITA's troops were training in Morocco, which was sympathetic to their cause and since the South Africans could not venture openly to Morocco, it was logical to use Affretair, particularly with Jack's background as a successful mercenary.

We flew from Waterkloof to Grootfontein, where Colin and his crew remained leaving me, George, and Dave, to fly directly to Rabat in Morocco where we collected well over 100 UNITA personnel. As before, there were no seats and the troops made themselves as comfortable as they could on the floor, while we re-adjusted the temperature in the hold for humans instead of carcasses. We flew directly back to Grootfontein, disregarding the airways and flying at non-standard altitudes. On the way north we flew directly over Angola without filing a flight plan until we were abeam Gabon where we initiated our flight plan as having departed from Libreville. On the return journey we employed the same tactic in reverse and once again abeam Libreville we cancelled our flight plan and flew directly over Angola without speaking to ATC until we landed back at Grootfontein. The troops debussed from the DC-8 and were immediately transported across the border to start their careers as guerrillas fighting for UNITA. Colin and his crew having been well rested then flew us back to base.

I finished off the month with a couple of Dakota flights; a pleasant change since I had not worked with 3 Squadron in over a month.

October to December

Affretair commitments and a handful of air force missions consumed the balance of the working year. It began with a trip up to Amsterdam through Jeddah and Zurich, followed by a long wait for a return flight, only to realise that a series of simulator checks made it sensible to stay put for around two weeks in Amsterdam.

At the end of the first week in November, I flew from Harare to Lubumbashi, Kinshasa, Cairo, and Amsterdam before popping across the channel to finally land legally in the UK at Stanstead. Another crew was already waiting to fly the aircraft south, so we spent the night in a very pleasant pub near Cambridge before flying back to Amsterdam the next day. The following day I operated back via Tunis, Libreville, and Johannesburg to spend a few days at home before returning to Europe at the end of the month, this time finishing the run in Shannon. Five years had passed since my last visit and the rest of the crew had never been there before, so we visited old haunts such as Durty Nelly's and Bunratty Castle for a pleasant few days. We were due to fly out of Dublin, so we hired a car and drove up through Ireland only to find the flight had been rescheduled and was now operating out of Shannon once more with stops in Palma and Libreville.

December started off with an air force night flying detail. On December 11 I was both lucky and sad to fly one of six Dakotas in tight formation to drop the entire SAS regiment for its final parachute jump prior to disbanding. A lone Dakota climbed to HALO height, releasing the specialist free-fall SAS operators, led by their revered Grahame Wilson, to fly one last time and join their static line comrades. It was a poignant day for all of us. I watched those familiar mushroom-shaped chutes drift peacefully to earth with their brave warriors suspended below. I could not prevent my thoughts turning to the many killed and wounded in a lost cause.

John Hodges' early retirement to South Africa had not worked in his favour which meant he was welcomed back into the Affretair family with open arms. He, George, Skitch, and I were positioned down to Johannesburg mid-month for another 'smersh' flight. We picked up the aeroplane in Johannesburg and flew a short hop across to Waterkloof to take aboard a cargo of military hardware, before flying to Libreville for a fuel stop and then onwards to unload at Rabat. Our mission complete, we welcomed a nigh stop in Las Palmas before continuing to Amsterdam the next day. John and I spent the next few days completing simulator checks before flying home in time for Christmas.

Christmas and New Year were memorable with our great friends the Pithey family staying for the duration. Having had a great celebration, we drove to Kariba where we picked up Jerry Lynch's boat, crossing the lake to camp in the Matusadona National Park for a few days, before returning home to welcome in the New Year together.

1980 was unquestionably a year to remember, though not for all the right reasons. From then on many of our lives would change irrevocably and forever. Across the country we collectively reeled from the shock of Britain having sold us down the river and in the process setting in motion the destruction of a once well run and beautiful country populated by inherently good people.

Things were changing fast; areas of our lovely city were now no-go areas guarded by heavily-armed former and probably (as I viewed them) current enemies. I had always maintained that if Mugabe got into power, I would have to leave because I believed there was no future in staying under the leadership of a tyrant dedicated to destruction.

I had applied for and been accepted as a direct entry captain to Saudia, the Saudi Arabian national airline, but first had to satisfy two conditions. I had to arrive with a US Federal Aviation Administration license endorsed with a Boeing 707 rating, and I could only join as a captain once I was 33 years old. 1981 therefore would be dedicated to selling off virtually all I owned to raise the necessary funds for, and gaining, a 707 rating.

Achieving 33 was, of course, a matter of patience.

Pictured clockwise: 1) A change of make-up. The DC-8 in Cargoman livery 1978. 2) And as Affretair, 1977. 3) Me and Rich Beaver format on the CL-44 flown by Paddy Hirst. This is the only airborne photo of either DC-8 at the time, 1980.

7246648 krif d
15.48
15186 hils nl
rca aug 10 0948
4-456 rh
good day to u
kindly pass following message to capt rodwell - guest in your
hotel :

capt ian rodwell
101340/08
to u and yr crew my grateful thanks - sincerely hope u were not too
tired on arrival but appreciate very much yr time-keeping.

regards mandir

well recvd pse?+

ok we will bibi

15186 hils nl

10.33
15186 hils nl
4-456 rh
good morning to u - can u confirm that capt. rodwell of air gabon
cargo booked into yr hotel last night?+

mompls
the

yes he did +

pse pass following message to him :

200820/07
good morning ian,
fantastic achievement - i cud not believe yr progress report. pse
convey my sincere appreciation and thanks to u and yr crew. very
sorry for the pressure put on u all on this particular flt. pse
do yr best to quell any inquisitiveness on yr flt planning, and
sincerely hope that yr unheralded arrival ams and at the hotel
did not inconvenience u - it was my mistake i shud have
thought of booking yr hotel accommodation.

rgds malloch

ok pse?+

Pictured clockwise: 1) Thanks from the Boss: Telegrams from Jack Malloch
spell out his gratitude for our efforts sent to the Schiphol Hotel in Amsterdam
1981. **2)** High and mighty. Another sanctions-breaking mission over the French
Alps, 1978.

Pictured clockwise: 1) The Boss. Jack Malloch chats with well-wishers prior to take off in his restored World War Two Spitfire. 2) Captain Jack Malloch with his beloved, newly refurbished Spitfire 1981. Sadly for all who knew him, and many who didn't, he would lose his life in it in a crash in March 1982.

CHAPTER 17

Adventures in
paradise—1981

January

The charter business had picked up considerably now that we were a bona fide cargo airline. It meant another busy month as many of our charters now took us through Las Palmas, both north and southbound. I had to position to Frankfurt early in the month for a charter to Las Palmas and back. Late in the month I also had the pleasure of flying into Cape Town, which as many know boasts one of the most beautiful settings in the world. While the aircraft was being loaded, I was able to catch up with my mother who had relocated to the Cape, and John and Ann Borejzso who had also left Zimbabwe and moved down south.

February, March

I was busy again with both months involving flights to Tunis, Zurich, Barcelona, Mvengue (Gabon), Kano (Nigeria), Las Palmas, Durban, Bulawayo, and Accra (Ghana) among the usual destinations of Libreville, and Johannesburg. Fuel was cheaper in Nigeria than Gabon which meant that southbound to either Johannesburg or base we would stop to refuel in Kano rather than Libreville. On the deck in Kano, while ground crew refuelled the aircraft we had to physically visit the control tower to file our onward flight plan and pay our landing fees since we had no resident agent to act for us. Invariably the office downstairs was unstaffed, and we would have to climb up the long, spiral metal staircase to the top of the tower, where the controllers operated. The tower itself lacked a toilet and the controllers, who could not be bothered to walk back downstairs, would relieve themselves by urinating down the metal stairway, leaving a sickening stench that made the filing of the flight plan an unwelcome task. Kano was never one of our favourite destinations.

By April our DC-8s were due for a spar modification and check having both reached the designated hours requiring this major mandatory maintenance. Most of the overhaul facilities able to carry out such technical work were based in Europe or the US and as such were very expensive. The company did its research and found that HAECO, the engineering subsidiary of the giant Swire corporation in Hong Kong, could carry out the necessary work at a reasonable price. I was fortunate enough to be allocated the initial flight and as we would be there for at least two weeks we were encouraged to take our wives. Apart from Brian Morrison and Cliff Hawthorne we had Mary Hawthorne, Jennifer, my wife, and Arnie Konsolas (who had come along for the ride) in the back as we set took off from base on a direct flight to Singapore for a night stop, a great social start to our trip.

A designated KLM instructor endorsed Brian and me to fly into Hong Kong, taking us through a session in the simulator before we left. Every pilot operating into Hong Kong's Kai Tak airport had to have such an endorsement prior to their first flight there. The instrument guidance system (IGS) approach onto runway 13 at Kai Tak is notoriously awkward and there were probably few pilots in the world who would not have wished to have flown the approach. Those who have share a special experience. Runway 13 was in use for our arrival and as usual the visibility was poor so we could not really see the city of Hong Kong until we were virtually over it. The IGS involves flying down an instrument landing system (ILS) that does not culminate in a runway but rather a red and white checkerboard painted onto a rock on the side of a mountain. Once you become visual with the runway, normally at about 800 feet because of the prevailing poor visibility, you will see the runway off to your right, projecting into the bay and surrounded by water on three sides. You have to bank the aircraft, turning through about 60 degrees, to align yourself with the runway centreline while descending beside blocks of flats adjacent to the approach path. It was an exhilarating and memorable event. Brian and I had no idea at the time that we would have the pleasure of flying that IGS hundreds of times in our later careers.

The hotel in which we initially stayed was the Miramar on Nathan Road in Kowloon, which is actually part of the Chinese mainland. It was a package tour hotel facility and we managed to move to the Excelsior Hotel on Victoria Island, the original heart of Hong Kong, a substantial improvement. It was a memorable and enjoyable introduction to that exotic, bustling city, included a fascinating guided tour laid on by HAECO into the New Territories on the Chinese border. A huge, heavily-guarded fence demarcated the actual border.

Hong Kong by then was a multicultural city though of course with an extensive Chinese cultural and culinary influence. The local food was like nothing we had ever tasted or experienced. Peking duck, beggar's chicken, chili shredded beef, and crispy seaweed were just a few of the delights in which we indulged ourselves. The quality and variety of the street food was amazing and to our pockets, accustomed to European prices, almost ridiculously cheap. After two weeks of tourist leisure we flew back to Amsterdam via Madras and Dubai before returning home.

May

We still flew regularly into Moroni on the Comoros Islands, carrying chilled meat inbound and fresh fish and seafood outbound. While the aircraft was unloaded and reloaded, we generally had at least two hours on the ground. The Indian Ocean lapped gently against the built-up runway opposite the parking apron. We developed a delightful routine, taking swimming costumes, goggles, and towels with us. We would stroll across the tarmac strip, climb down the volcanic rocks to the water's edge and plunge into the gentle swell. A tropical wonderland would greet us as we immersed our faces. An hour would flash by in this hallucinogenic aquarium before we emerged, changed, and wandered back to the aircraft. The contrast between the almost comic, child-like splendour of this underwater lightshow, and the clinical technology of the cockpit—so close together—seemed both brilliant and bizarre.

One weekend our boys invited their friend, Johnnie, over to stay. On the Saturday evening before I was due to fly to Moroni the next morning, I phoned our duty manager and asked for four passenger tickets to take some children with me on the trip, having first phoned Johnnie's parents to seek their approval. Both requests were granted and keeping the trip as a surprise I packed a bag with towels, swimmers, and goggles, and woke the boys at 4am instructing them to dress warmly in preparation for an adventure. No passports were necessary because we went directly from the car into the aeroplane. My lads had been in the aircraft before on holiday to Europe but for nine or ten-year-old Johnnie, this was a startling and thrilling first. We flew to Moroni, disembarked, and within minutes were swimming in the sea. Coming from land-locked Zimbabwe, the children had never been exposed to the visual feast of brilliantly coloured tropical fish swimming serenely all around them. The joy on their excited faces etched itself onto my heart forever.

We flew home in time for a lunchtime *braai* for lunch with the kids chattering animatedly about their adventure. The next day at school the teacher asked each of the children what they had done over the weekend, receiving the usual accounts of everyday activities at home. When she came to Johnnie, he disgorged a fantasy involving a huge jet aircraft, a remote tropical island, and floating in azure seas among paradisal sea life. After class the teacher asked to see his mother. Along with suggestions of Johnnie's over-vivid imagination, she asked if everything was alright at home. His mother smiled and replied, 'Yes, and he was telling the truth.'

June began with my conducting an air test to approve a control repair on the LVK, the Gabonese-registered DC-8, along with Roger Brackley and John Hodges. Once we had completed the exercise I radioed the tower for permission to fly a low pass over the airport as I knew some of the ground staff were keen to take photographs. As we commenced our approach, originally planned for the main runway, the tower warned us that an Air Zimbabwe Viscount had just landed and was still on the strip. As we were flying at about 300 knots, we adjusted our direction slightly and flew along the taxiway in front of the terminal, dropping to as low as 10 feet on the radio altimeter at one point. We could still have that sort of fun in those days.

The DC-8 flying during the month included trips to Nairobi, Zurich, Luanda and, of all places, Lusaka airport, the scene of my teen-aged war hero escapade.

To keep my air force category and currency valid, I undertook my Master Green rating renewal in the middle of the month which was nerve wracking but also enjoyably challenging.

The other co-pilots qualified on the DC-7 were military ranked who did not have a civilian license, or if they did, needed to convert it to an airline transport pilot license (ATPL) in order to upgrade to captain on type. George Alexander, who had now taken over as the DC-7 pilot manager, wanted another qualified captain on type. He asked Boss Jack if he could supervise my conversion flights. Jack agreed, leading to my undertaking a series of upgrade flights, including four to Blantyre (Malawi) and back as part of my training. Flying with George and John Hodges as the flight engineer put me in excellent hands and made the whole process straightforward.

Apart from a quick instrument rating renewal trip for John Fleming and Mike Gibson, I flew the rest of July with an ex air force colleague, Chris Abrams, who had recently joined Affretair. We flew an operation through Douala in Cameroon to Amsterdam and back before we were tasked on another smersh mission with John Hodges and Skitch. Once again, we positioned down to Johannesburg for a night stop before picking up the aeroplane and flying across to Waterkloof to collect more military hardware which we flew once more to Rabat via Libreville. Once we had off-loaded in Rabat, we continued to Amsterdam and resumed normal duties.

During the year I had been trying to convert many of my belongings into hard cash in order to pay for my Boeing 707 course and Chris had been very successful in converting local currency into pounds sterling by auctioning Rhodesian stamps in the London auction houses. He kindly helped me do the same and I soon built up a reasonable portfolio. The foreign currency restrictions introduced by the Rhodesian Government were still enforced and residents could take a maximum of only US$1,000 out of the country. As my course was going to cost US$28,000, I was stuck.

However, I applied to the exchange control authorities, submitting the breakdown of my course costs, and suggesting that my request should be approved. I based my rationale on the benefits my further aviation qualifications would bring to Zimbabwe, pointing out that Air Zimbabwe already had a small fleet of Boeing 707s. Amazingly, the foreign currency desk approved my request; now all I had to do was raise the money.

The payment process was bureaucratic and complex. Once I had secured my place on the course with ATI, an air training organisation in San Mateo outside San Francisco, I had to transfer the funds to the Foreign Affairs Department who in turn transferred the funds to ATI. They deemed it necessary to prevent my leaving the country with more funds than were allowed.

Apart from a night-flying and para-dropping exercise with 3 Squadron, the rest of August's flying was on the DC-8, with another identical smersh trip from Waterkloof to Rabat carrying arms, munitions, and other military hardware. We followed up with three trips to Amsterdam during the rest of the month, once via Lagos.

September saw one flight with 3 Squadron prior to operations to Amsterdam and back through Luanda, Palma, Libreville, and Johannesburg. Phil Palmer from the DCA accompanied me to refamiliarize on the DC-8 as he hadn't flown it for some time. The month continued with George and my upgrade training on the DC-7 on flights to Lubumbashi (DRC), Ndola (Zambia), and Blantyre (Malawi). A meat delivery to Zurich before continuing to Amsterdam and then back home wound up the month.

October started off with another meat run to Zurich and then up to Amsterdam before returning. However, on the sector into Libreville we experienced a hydraulic failure which necessitated us refuelling there and back-tracking to Amsterdam to have a spare part fitted. Luckily, once again I was in the hands of master flight engineer, John Hodges, whose management of the failure was flawless.

Mid-month, George continued with my line training on the DC-7 with flights to Lubumbashi and Ndola which represented my final check out. I was now a captain on the DC-7, a marvellous sensation as it was such an iconic old aeroplane. We flew together with John on a smersh mission to Waterkloof before proceeding on to Durban where we night stopped, having a memorable celebration of our time together. The next morning on our return to base we again requested a low level VFR departure and were subsequently cleared to proceed not above 2,500 feet until we had exited the Durban area control centre (ACC) boundary. For us it was magic hugging the coastline, and for spectators on the ground it must have been a sight to behold— this beautiful, huge, piston-engine aircraft flying past at such a dramatically low level.

I took the liberty of turning to fly as low as I dared over Salt Rock where the Pitheys lived and where we had holidayed a couple of years before. I look back on my time flying the DC-7 with great appreciation and nostalgia. I did not know then this was my last flight in that magnificent machine.

The following week was taken up with formation practice in the DC-3. The air force planned an air display for the general public, with the event well attended in late November.

November was another personally historic, nostalgic, and sad month for me. I flew two sorties on the Dakota, unaware that my excursion with Clive Ward on November 21 would be not only my last flight with 3 Squadron but also the last time I would ever pilot the mighty DC-3 I had grown to love.

One trip to Europe on the DC-8, including two covert trips into Lubumbashi with Chris and John, made up the rest of the month.

Saudia, the Saudi Arabian airline had confirmed my start date for the beginning of March. Now came the heart-breaking task of tendering my resignation. A formal letter was necessary, but I was equally aware I had to have a face-to-face exchange with Boss Jack. On my way to work one morning I had stopped off for petrol and Jack drew up next to me in his big American car. I had left a message with Nori Mann, Jack's long-term and loyal secretary, asking for an appointment, but now seemed a better opportunity rather than in the confines of his office. I told him I was leaving, and I am sure it came as no surprise; many of his pilots and staff were also emigrating in search of a more certain future.

We never had an intimate relationship. I was his junior by nearly 30 years but having flown together on many occasions, a mutual respect had developed between us. I think he was probably annoyed at losing a pilot in whom the airline had invested so much training. But he thanked me for all I had done and wished me every success in the future. Once more, I did not know then that this would be my last meeting with this legend of a man and pilot whom we all loved and revered.

The year concluded with two flights to Europe and back visiting Accra, Kano, Amsterdam, and Munich and touching down at home on Christmas day.

On Boxing day, I cadged a lift on the DC-8 to Amsterdam before flying with KLM to San Francisco to start my Boeing 707 conversion course. I successfully completed it in early February, acquiring an FAA ATP (Airline Transport Pilot) licence in the process.

CHAPTER EIGHTEEN

An era ends—1982

T he Boeing 707 course was an eye opener. My instructors were all experienced former Pan Am or Trans World Airlines pilots who were casual but professional and I managed to complete the course with money to spare which after a year or two was refunded. It meant I actually got more foreign currency out of Zimbabwe than was allowed at the time.

I always found Douglas-manufactured aircraft a delight to fly. The DC-8 compared to the 707 has a clean wing with no strakes (aerodynamic ridges) to assist the airflow. The DC-8 flight controls were so light and well harmonised, whereas my first experience in trying to turn the 707 was a shock; you needed so much more muscle to move the controls. The DC-8 would, at the correct speed, easily lift into the air on take-off, whereas you had to almost literally drag the 707 off the ground.

However, I concede that the basic Boeing systems—electrics, fuel, and hydraulics—seemed more logical to grasp and operate. Still, they were fabulous aircraft of their era, and I have been lucky to fly many hours on both.

I flew from the US course to Amsterdam to undergo some checks in the DC-8 simulator before flying home. Three pilots were going through their command upgrade on the DC-8 having served as captains on the Affretair Canadair turbo prop CL-44. Sam Richman and I flew back up to Amsterdam to complete their simulator part of the upgrade before flying back to base on February 21 1982. It was my last flight on the DC-8, and with Affretair.

Epilogue

Not so many of us remain to tell a story of their involvement in the demise of Rhodesia. I do not deny history or the need for justice and human rights. If I have an argument, it is with the morals and methods of those pursuing these ends, and the barely-disguised cynicism with which they went about achieving them.

Was I lucky to have been part of that story? No, I do not believe so. My presence was more by default than by choice. But I could not abandon this beautiful country and her proud people who came to Britain's aid in her hour of need. On countless occasions they gave their lives for the love of a distant motherland.

In return, I felt Britain had forsaken these loyal subjects in their own time of desperate need. My sense of duty was stronger than my desire to avoid what was no doubt an inevitable catastrophe. The obligation to defend our principles when so many of my generation fled leaving their parents to suffer through the war was overpowering.

Every participant on both sides of the conflict suffered. As a combatant, I was fortunate not only to survive, but to come through at least physically uninjured. But I was not immune to the stresses of war. My marriage broke up, as did hundreds of others. The best I can say to my first wife, Jennifer, is I am sorry it failed to work out.

For the past year I lived on a farm well out of town with the kind and gentle Nicky, Affretair's much-loved operations assistant, with whom in time I was to have a son, Scott.

But now I could no longer live in the country for which I had been prepared to give my life. To this day the reality, but not my decision, remains a powerful regret.

I have said before I am no hero. I merely did what was necessary and possibly a little more. I was proud to have won acceptance into a family of incredibly brave people. They fought to the last trying to protect a country from itself in a war they were never going to be allowed to win. A more valiant group of soldiers and aircrew arguably does not exist. The pride that glows within me in that cause outweighs my feelings to the contrary, even conceding the inevitable march of history.

To have flown for Affretair and worked for and with Jack Malloch as well as the tremendous personalities with whom I was lucky enough to forge a subsequently long and rewarding aviation career is one of the greatest privileges of my life.

In March 1982 I left my beloved country. I was 33 years old, younger than all of my children today. I had two suitcases and $20 in my pocket to embark upon a new life. But that is another story.

The end

Appendix

I ts origins remain obscure but there is a certain truth in the saying sometimes attributed to Winston Churchill: history is written by the victors. The Rhodesian bush war suffers no shortage of historic analysis, fought as it was under the global glare of largely hostile media eager to see the demise of white minority rule.

Nor does it lack memoirs, biographies, and other personal accounts of participants. Paradoxically, the balance in terms of sheer volume of documented accounts swings substantially to combatants on the losing side of the political divide.

This imbalance has several explanations, the most cogent of which is that the Rhodesian security forces knew they were not defeated on the battleground. Rather, they had to bow to sustained local and international political and economic pressure.

In writing my account of my part in this era, I have attempted at all times to present only issues and events as I saw and experienced them. In order to reflect that personal approach, I include here an excerpt from the history of the Rhodesian Air Force No 1 Parachute Training school. The extract mentions my role in two of the operations into Zambia and Mozambique. I incorporate it here unchanged to give readers a comparative account of some of the action from a third party perspective.

High Above & Far Beyond

The History of the Rhodesian Airforce no.1 Parachute Training School

Showing posts sorted by date for query rodwell.
Sort by relevance. Show all posts Wednesday, 8 November 2017.

Chapter 31
Operation Gatling: Revenge for the Viscount Airline Disaster

Only in Rhodesia would a paratrooper qualify for his wings with an operational jump, into action, deep in a hostile country. Only in Rhodesia would troops be forced to scrounge, beg and borrow equipment for a major military operation. Only in Rhodesia would we send a few hundred paratroops to attack over 4000 enemy in camps hundreds of kilometres apart, not once, but twice in one day. But desperate times call for desperate measures. And we were desperately seeking revenge.

On 3rd September 1978 at 17h10 a civilian Viscount Airliner took off from Kariba Airport and headed for Salisbury. There were 58 civilian passengers and crew on board, mostly holiday makers. Approximately 5 mins after take-off, and just as the Captain turned onto the heading for Salisbury, a SAM 7 heat seeking missile struck the inner starboard turbo prop engine. The pilot, Captain John Hood, immediately put out a Mayday radio call and, fighting for control, managed to put the stricken Viscount into a shallow dive. The starboard wing was on fire and the captain had no choice but to crash land.

As the aircraft approached the ground Captain Hood saw a clearing ahead and, with great skill, managed to land his plane there. Unfortunately there was a large ditch across it and the Viscount broke up on impact. 18 passengers in the tail section, some severely injured, survived the crash and made their way clear of the wreckage.

The Rhodesian Air Force immediately sent out search and rescue aircraft to the area, but it was not until the next morning the wreckage was found by a Dakota with SAS paratroopers on board. The skipper, Flt/Lt Nick Mehmel, a reserve pilot, dropped the paratroopers onto the smouldering wreckage.

As the SAS floated down they saw a group of bodies who'd clearly escaped the crash. They were horrified to discover these survivors were murdered - killed by the group of terrorists who'd shot down the plane. Three survivors escaped when the terrorists opened fire, by running into the bush, and five others, who'd gone to seek help, remained hidden.

Of the 18 people who survived the shooting down of what was clearly a civilian passenger aircraft, 10 had been murdered. Two of these were little girls aged 11 and 4. The terrorist gang involved in this outrageous massacre were from the ZIPRA faction lead by Joshua Nkomo, and had crossed into Rhodesia from Zambia.

There was a deafening silence from the rest of the world, not a single country apart from the Republic of South Africa, uttered one word of condemnation. This left a bitter and angry Rhodesia little choice – revenge and retribution was the only option.

We had to teach them a real lesson, as the RLI said, "Let's cull the bastards." Our desire for action was fueled [sic] by the blatant bragging to the International press, of ZIPRA leader, Joshua Nkomo. He happily claimed responsibility for shooting down the plane, but then plead ignorance over the murder of the survivors. We were determined to hit back hard and annihilate the animals who slaughtered innocent children.

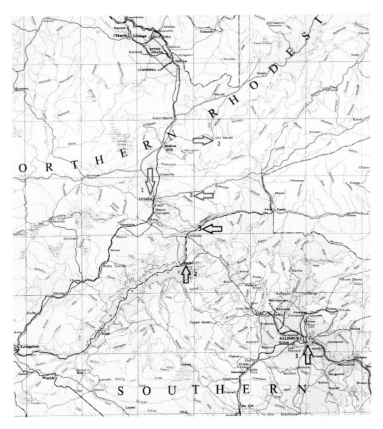

The above map shows the start points (in black) for the attacks on the terrorist bases in Zambia. The black arrow with the #1 was the New Sarum Air Base from which the Canberra B2 bombers laid waste to the FC Terrorist camp, red arrow #1, and also took control of Zambian air space. New Sarum was also the start point for the vertical envelopment of the Terrorist camp at Mkushi red arrow #2. The DC7F also started from New Sarum and their drop of men, fuel drums and ammunition into the Admin base situated only a 5 to 6 min chopper flight south of the Mkushi camp. The last terrorist camp to be hit was the CGT 2 (Communist Guerrilla Training 2) at red arrow 3 and the start point for the RLI paratroopers who vertically enveloped this target was FAF2 at Kariba airfield, black arrow 2. Black arrow 3 at Mana Pools was the start point for the helicopter borne SAS attack on the Mkushi camp red arrow 2 and also for the RLI helicopter men who hit CGT2 red arrow 3. The helicopter gun ships (K car) also attacked all 3 targets and their start point was also from black arrow 3. I believe hundreds of terrorists and maybe thousands were killed in these attacks. Unfortunately one SAS trooper was killed at Mkushi, where a bushfire also destroyed some of our parachutes. The attack on CGT2 was a lemon and the RLI found that most of the terrorists had wisely departed in a hurry.

HEADWIND: AN AFRICAN AIR ODYSSEY

And, on 19th October 1978 we took revenge in a massive way. We hit three separate camps, deep inside Zambia, where the terrorists thought they were safe. The first strike was on the main terrorist base known as Freedom Camp (FC), 15kms outside Lusaka the Zambian capital. It contained 4000 terrorists under training, as well as the ZIPRA military high command. This attack was a pure airstrike involving Hunter FB9, Canberra B2 and Alouette III K car gunships and it struck at 08.30hrs when the terrorists were on parade. In this famous attack Green Leader, Canberra Bomber Section leader, Sqn/Ldr Chris Dixon, took control of Zambian Airspace, thousands of terrorists were culled and a Rhodesian icon was born.

The second attack was a vertical envelopment of Mkushi Camp, conducted by the SAS, and took place immediately after the attack on FC Camp. 125 kilometres North East of Lusaka, this camp contained approximately 1000 terrorists. They knew they were in for a beating when the massive explosions, delivered by the Hunters and Canberra B2 Bombers, enveloped them.

Ground shaking explosions were followed by the devastating chatter of cannon fire from the Allouette III helicopter gunships. Then, as the remaining terrorists began to run for it, they were confronted by our men, floating down by parachute. They knew their time had come.

This photograph shows that every SAS soldier was used on these raids. It would have been nearly impossible to stop Sgt Major Jock Hutt0n from jumping on this operation. He is seen here in his usual relaxed manner waiting to be checked by the PJI dispatchers and wearing his combat cap. His stories about his jump into Normandy on D day WW2 were always very amusing especially when told in his broad Scots accent.

Paratroops were also dropped onto an Admin Base close to the Mkushi camp to ready the helicopter fuel and ammunition dropped by a DC7. This drop was onto what appeared to be nice, open, grass- land and indeed it was. But there was a snag - it was covered in what is known as Buffalo Beans, a creeper which grows beans covered in fine hairs which pierce the skin and cause very painful itching. The only way to prevent the extremely uncomfortable scratching is to plaster the affected area with mud. Once it dries it can be peeled off to remove the hairs with it. These guys cursed us mightily for the DZ selection. (So did the parachute packers, who, after the chutes were returned, had to deal with an unexpected shower of Buffalo Beans as they checked and repacked them. (We were very unpopular for a long time over this.)

The troops who jumped into this admin base included the retired RSM of the SAS, Stan Standish, who had somehow managed to wangle his way onto this operation. In his late 60s at the time, Stan was the oldest person to carry out an operational parachute jump in Rhodesia, and probably the world. He had jumped at Arnhem during WW2, over 30 years before. When asked if there was anyone older he replied, "Only the Bloody Aircraft." Every member of the SAS was used on this attack, every plane was used and every PJI was also called up. Stan, the legend, was certainly not going to miss out!

The third attack was also a vertical envelopment, this time of the CGT2 complex (Communist Guerrilla Training) approximately 100 kilometres South East of Lusaka. This complex also housed many thousands of terrorists.

This time the approximately 168 paratroopers were drawn from the RLI. 60 of these were on a Basic RLI static line course going through the Parachute Training School at the time. Immediately after their 7th jump (the night jump) they were to return to barracks to ready for their qualifying wings jump the next morning. Instead the trucks turned off and they found themselves at the SAS Kabrit Barracks where they were quarantined.

It was here they were told their final qualifying jump would not exactly be standard. They would only get their wings after they had completed an operational jump. Into action. Deep in hostile territory. They were truly going to earn their wings!

Next day these men returned to PTS, drew their full battle loads, and found a large amount of additional equipment, including extra MAG belted 7.62 mm ammunition, RPG 7 rocket launchers 60mm mortars and bombs, and extra A63 radios and batteries. This meant almost every paratrooper was carrying a suspended load which was not usual in the Fire Force Role.

Unlike the SAS, the RLI did not have the equipment to make up the suspended loads. The RLI had not thought about the CSPEP (carrying straps personal equipment parachutist). Or jettison devices. Or suspension ropes. Or suspension hooks.

These troops learned to jump with loads using the training equipment provided by PTS. They knew how to use it and had used it, but now, it appeared, there was none available from their own resources. Only the SAS had this equipment and they were fully committed to the attack on Mkushi. In the end, the RLI used the training equipment from PTS.

The RLI collected their equipment and were taken up to the PTS hangar where they found the usual incredibly detailed models of the targets. They were also informed that this attack was the final of three and would only take place after the other two had been hit.

This meant one of three possible scenarios would greet them; the enemy might be forewarned because of the two previous attacks and abandon the complex; they could be forewarned but stand and fight, which could make the day a very messy affair; or they could be totally ignorant of the previous attacks and get a serious surprise. Obviously we were hoping for the third option.

The RLI were positioned at FAF2 Kariba for their start point. As soon as the briefing was over these 160-ish RLI, including the 60 not yet qualified paratroopers, went to Safety Equipment Section and drew their parachutes. They packed their kit into the suspended loads and the PJIs distributed our CSPEPS amongst them. Then more problems emerged - there just was not enough equipment to go around.

I hurried down to Safety Equipment Section where rolls of webbing were used to repair parachute harnesses and seat belts. There was also a supply of knurled buckles from the original weapons containers we had discarded many years before. In Rhodesia, during these times absolutely nothing was thrown away, and we were the masters of recycling. Also available were D rings. All these items could be attached to the webbing with heavy duty sewing machines in the repair shop. There was light grade canvas material and some sensible fellows had their ponchos. By sewing two lengths of webbing together in the form of a cross then placing a piece of canvas or a poncho over the webbing and piling all the kit into the middle we were able to tie this up like a parcel. This now became a suspended load. Not the best, not the safest, but under the circumstances it was all we could do.

However this was not the end of the troubles. We didn't have enough suspension ropes or jettison devices, and we were also short of quick release hooks. Normally when a paratrooper jumped with a suspended load it was attached to the two lower D rings on the parachute harness with two quick release hooks. After the parachute deployed, the levers on the quick release hooks operated, permitting the load to drop to the end of the suspension rope. The rope was fitted with a jettison device in case of a parachute malfunction. If the paratrooper jettisoned his load he would be useless in the forthcoming battle because his equipment would be smashed.

I decided no paratrooper jumping on this operation was to jettison his equipment. Result, we did not need a jettison device, only a piece of suitable rope about 5mt long, one end tied to the bundle and the other to the parachute harness.

When they jumped, all soldiers would carry their personal weapon attached to their body with a fully loaded magazine on the rifle or with a

50 round belt fitted to the MAG – ready to use immediately. They would also have their usual webbing under the parachute harness with the usual allocation of water bottles, grenades, ten full rifle magazines and wound dressing etc.

For a few years PTS had tried out various, locally made items of equipment. One such item was rope for the replacement of the suspension rope we normally used, which could only be obtained outside the country. However, all the ropes we tested broke when we dropped loads from the fan platform in the PTS hangar and the salesman was sent on his way.

Now, all of a sudden the smelly stuff was hitting the fan, we needed rope, lots of it. I visited Safety Equipment Section and obtained a roll of parachute rigging line with a supposed breaking strain of 500lbs. Perhaps if doubled up it would be OK. For the quick release hooks we had only one option, instead of two hooks per paratrooper with a suspended load, they would have one and would just have to hang onto their loads until after parachute deployment. This was what was known as an operational necessity.

I'd just fitted my own weapon and parachute when the commander of the Air Force personally came to ask how it was going. Although we'd been doing it for years, this was the only time this particular Commander ever bothered to see us off. We were about to dispatch over 300 paratroopers onto two different targets and an admin base and we did not have the correct gear. How the hell did he think I was going?

I let him have it with both barrels. What we were doing, even with all the necessaries, was ambitious and risky - without the proper equipment it was, to put it mildly, fucking dangerous. There was a good chance some of these teenage soldiers would be killed due simply to equipment failure. Just maybe we were doing one jump too many. I stomped off and joined my stick. Not the way to win friends or to gain promotion.

As it turned out not a single parachuting injury occurred on this operation and after the battles were over PTS got almost all its equipment back. This was testimony to the training the troops received and their discipline under the most stressful circumstances.

The operational plan called for Dakotas to fly the RLI into FAF2 at Kariba early the following morning. The planes would then return to New Sarum, pick up the SAS, drop them onto the Mkushi complex, return to FAF2 Kariba as soon as possible, pick up the RLI and drop them onto CGT2 camp. In the mean- time the Hunters and Canberras were re-armed for their third strike and would hit this camp in the usual way, just before the parachutists dropped. We did not have many aircraft or many PJIs – every single one was used on each of the three attacks so this was also a highly structured, and for all involved highly exhausting, logistical operation.

Another 48 RLI troops were dropped by Alouette III helicopters from their forward base at Mana Pools, just south of the Zambezi. There were also 4 Allouette K car gunships. The ground commander was in one to control the battle as was usual in a Fire Force type strike. In addition to the K car gunships there were Vampire and Lynx aircraft available overhead for heavy ground support if required.

After the drop onto Mkushi terrorist base camp, the Dakotas flew at very low level back to Rhodesia and crossed the Zambezi River to land at the FAF2, where the RLI waited already kitted up. The Dakotas re-fueled [sic] and immediately loaded the RLI paratroopers. Before climbing aboard I gave them the Gypsy's warning about refusing to jump.

Then we were airborne again heading into a very hostile Zambia. The Skipper was Flt/Lt Rodwell the youngest Volunteer Reserve Dakota Captain.

Immediately after the drop on CGT2 camp the Dakotas returned to FAF2 base where they were refuelled and given the once over by the techs. The FAF commander organised a magnificent spread and it was only then I realised I'd only drunk coffee for the last 24hrs and most of my PJIs were in the same boat. Tony Hughes piled his plate up with cold meats and salads and topped it off with a scoop of ice cream. He just wanted food and did not care in what order it arrived in his stomach.

But our day was not yet over. We loaded a Dakota with 200ltr drums of helicopter fuel and fitted them with parachutes in case they were needed. Sometime around 4pm that afternoon, as the paratroopers were withdrawn by helicopter, the call for fuel came into the FAF2 Ops room and the Dakota, with the drums on board, flew off with a couple of PJI s on board to shove them out the door.

The reason for the PJIs doing this was because 3 Air Supply Platoon were fully committed with the DC7 dropping stuff into the Admin Base. A couple of the U/T PJIs provided the muscle with a qualified PJI in command for this task, and they had a very exciting trip. On their way back they were hazed by a Zambian training jet of Russian make. The Dakota headed for the trees and flew very low. Fortunately this Jet decided discretion was the better part of valour when faced with a Hunter FB9 carrying side-winder air to air missiles.

After the attack most of the parachutes were recovered as well as the CSPEP equipment belonging to PTS. In fact, whenever we carried out these raids, nearly all of the parachuting equipment was recovered. This was due to the dedication and care of the young soldiers who'd jumped and was a significant bonus for a country affected by sanctions.

Operation Gatling was an outstanding success despite the shortage of equipment. The air strike on the FC camp killed thousands of terrorists and wounded many more. The vertical envelopment of Mkushi camp also resulted in many hundreds of terrorists killed, including many armed and camouflaged women. This camp was totally destroyed. The third attack on the CTG2 complex yielded only about fifty terrorists because the bulk of the terrorists had wisely abandoned the place. Both camps attacked by paratroopers were ambushed over-night. The next morning the SAS were confronted by the Zambian Army accompanied by ZIPRA terrorists, and in the fire fight that ensued, the enemy were obliterated without loss to the SAS.

As soon as the Dakota doing the resupply drop returned, I looked for a place to put my head down. I had spent over 11 hours 30 minutes in the back of a Dakota and, before this, many hours planning and preparing. I, like all involved, was mentally and physically wrecked. But adrenalin was still high and this was not about to happen. Especially when the Army Intelligence officer convinced us it would be splendid to visit the casino and give the local population a morale boost.

By this time news of this successful operation had hit the news – thousands of terrorists killed, their bases annihilated and all without a single loss on our side. Needless to say, at the casino we were treated like celebrities and given free drinks for the rest of the night.

My host for the night was a territorial officer who was well known at the casino, and an expert at roulette. I did not know how to play, but borrowed $10 from one of the guards at FAF2. After watching my expert, I placed a few bets and won. I put the $10 worth of chips I'd borrowed into my boot top and played with the chips I'd just won. In the end I won a substantial amount of money which was all spent the next day on a party with the RLI, especially for the young, newly qualified paratroopers.

As it turns out, this is how the entire operation went – we took a gamble with the few bits and pieces of equipment we managed to scrounge together, and won big. But it was not such a great risk because we were relying on well-trained, very determined, and very brave men who had a massive thirst for revenge. We were always going to win this one.

Chapter 23
Selous Scout Operations in Gaza Province Mozambique

Gaza Province, Mozambique, is flat and featureless, hard territory to accurately navigate with our usual, head-out-the-door method. Many HALO operations were carried out into this part of Mozambique and it was always very difficult to get clearly visible, and identifiable navigation points.

The usual preferred points were river beds especially during the dry season when the white sand was easily seen even on dark nights but in this flat, arid part of Africa, it was not always possible. Water in this part of the world, is scarce, and most available sources are surrounded by inhabitants. For this reason, every HALO drop was carried out with a HALO box loaded up with water.

Occasionally we would fly into our target by using points on the Limpopo River which meant we inadvertently invaded South African air space. Fortunately for us they did not investigate these intrusions with a couple of jet fighters. We also used the power line, supplying the South Africans with power generated at the giant Cabora Bassa Dam on the Zambezi River as a guide. But many a drop was done simply by setting a stop watch at a given reference point, flying for a certain amount of time, and, as long as there was no obvious habitation, out the stick would go.

After we obtained KAP3 automatic opening devices we were not restricted to 15,000ft AGL – we could go higher or lower depending on the situation or the clouds.

On one of these HALO operations with the Selous Scouts, we carried out the highest operational freefall drop in our conflict. Dennis Crocamp [sic] jumped from as high as the Dakota would go that night– 26,000ft AGL. It would have taken up to 120 seconds to reach the ground from that height. Well done, Dennis. You are a legend! There was no particular reason for going that high on this particular night except that it was beautiful and clear, and for once the navigation points on the Save River were easily visible.

But we did not always go in at high altitude. In fact, dropping static line troops into this featureless country on a moonless night could only be done by flying very low, low enough that we could make out features against a dim horizon, and low enough that we would become a too fast target for enemy fire. In other words, about 50ft AGL – not much higher than the tree-tops.

We knew the countryside in this area was billiard-table flat and enabled extremely low flight. In addition we were trying to insert paratroops in the most clandestine way possible and the Dakota was much less of a target at treetop height when flying at 150 knots airspeed. On a dark night the Dakota was difficult to see, and, at such low height and such speed, we would pass before the enemy could react. Or so we assumed and hoped.

On one occasion we had a full load of Selous Scouts, all dressed like the enemy they planned to kill. The pilot was a volunteer Reserve Dakota Captain called Ian Rodwell. His day job was to fly for Jack Malloch's sanctions-busting freight airline AFFRETAIR as a DC8 Captain.

I tagged along to see how the PTS staff members were getting along and as usual, was armed to the teeth, and wearing a SAVIAC Free Fall rig, just in case. It would have been absolutely useless at this low altitude, but it just felt comfortable. It was a dark night and I was very surprised, and not a little bit terrified, that we did not climb at all but stayed right on the deck. Extremely low.

Even though I was up front between the pilots and looking directly out of the windscreen I could just make out the horizon, and barely read the dulled instrument lights. The door from the cockpit to the cabin was closed, because the PJI and dispatchers needed a little light to check the parachutes. As we thundered along at 150 knots, less than 50 feet above the trees, we could see any high ground or taller trees against a very faint horizon. Sporadically, the Skipper turned the landing lights on to check the height above the trees – a mere few feet. It made the heart beat faster and my sphincter muscles attempted to pinch a hole in my jocks – literally skimming the landscape does that to you!

After what seemed an eternity, but was probably only about an hour and a half, the Skipper told the dispatchers we were10 minutes out. The troops were stood up to check equipment and sound off, the cabin lights snuffed from dim to out and the stick brought to action stations. The Skipper hauled the aircraft up to 500 feet, put down the half-flap, cut the speed to 95 knots, and as soon as everything was nice and steady, called for the red light and a few seconds later the green. The troops went out, the dispatchers hauled in the bags and we turned to starboard, and the difficult part of the operation.

First we had to ensure the troops had landed safely, so we orbited a few miles away until we got the all clear. But as we orbited, we slowly lost altitude until we were back at 50 feet. For me, this was the scariest part of the whole operation.

After the stick was dispatched, we would, on many occasions, fly on a bit further and wake up the populace by chucking out a half-dozen ALPHA bouncing bombs. The purpose was not to cause death and destruction, but to make a loud, and terrifying noise to distract attention from the paratroops. Whether this was successful or not, who knows, but it seemed like a good plan at the time.

The Rhodesian ALPHA bomb was round and consisted of an inner steel case filled with explosive activated by an all way detonator with a half second delay. The inner case was surrounded by a larger outer steel case and the gap between the two was filled with high bounce rubber. When dropped the bomb would bounce into the air before exploding. This was a very effective noise-maker when three hundred were dropped at a time from a Canberra flying at 50 ft at 300 knots air speed.

After checking all the troops had arrived safely the only thing left was to see if we could find somewhere to drop a few ALPHA bouncing bombs. We were told at the briefing if we saw anything on our return flight, up the railway line from Jorge do Limpopo toward the border, we were free to throw these bombs at it. However, we were to make sure we did not get too close to Malvernia, the village on the Mozambique side of the border as the Ters and their Frelemo [*sic*] supporters had assembled a lot of anti-aircraft stuff in that area.

Of course, as it happens, we did see something on the line and decided to give it a go. The guys in the back got the bombs ready, a simple matter of pulling out a safety pin, and on word from the Skipper, tossed them out the door. It was a casual, if inaccurate, way of doing things, and possibly, a dangerous pastime. But hey, it was good fun and we might actually hit a bridge or something – flukes do happen in war, after all.

Whilst the men were arming the bombs, it suddenly dawned on me. If we dropped them out of the back door at 50 feet AGL with 150 knots on the clock, and considering they bounced before explosion, there was a good chance we would be in the danger area. Even at the Dakota's top speed, it was dicey. And to bomb ourselves out of the sky was not a desired outcome. So Ian Rodwell wound the elastic bands a bit tighter and shoved the throttles to the stops. The air-speed indicator moved to 200 knots and just as the target disappeared under the nose, Ian told the guys to "drop 'em."

Out the bombs went – six of the bright red round things. Then there was a loud bang about half-way along the fuselage and the sky was full of little green things which flashed past at tremendous speed. We'd stirred a hornets' nest with a big stick and taken a couple of hits from either 12.7mm or 14.5mm anti-aircraft fire. Fortunately they seemed to hone in on one casualty only; the Aircraft Engineer's toolbox. The most frightening thing about taking fire whilst in the rear of a Dakota was that there was nowhere to hide. You just had to grit your teeth and take it. The pilots up front were protected by having armour plated seats.

We decided discretion was the greater part of valour, and headed for Buffalo Range airfield with the Dakota's tail tucked firmly beneath the under carriage. Fortunately, nothing serious was damaged. We landed okay and taxied in to our dispersal without incident. It was only after the engines shut down that we discovered the batteries had taken a couple of hits. A replacement Dakota was sent down whilst the battle-scarred one entered rehabilitation.

This photograph is of Sgt Mike Wiltshire (PJI extraordinaire) with that determined look on his face. The go to man on the PTS staff if you wanted anything fixed, stolen or just made he would find a way to do almost anything.

To start the broken Dakota we needed a 24 volt DC power supply, and because the battery compartment was a shambles we had to repair it in the bush. A Dakota engineer removed the broken pieces of battery and managed to make the electrical connections safe, while Mike Wiltshire (PJI extraordinaire), skilfully connected two Land Rover batteries together, and started the engines so we could fly to New Sarum for proper repairs.

We were lucky on this occasion, but as the saying goes; God looks after drunks and fools.

https://highabovefarbeyond.blogspot.com/search?q=rodwell&max-results=20&by-date=true

Glossary of terms and abbreviations

ACC: Area control centre, administered by air traffic control.

ADF: Automatic direction finder.

ADI: Attitude direction indicator.

AH: Artificial horizon.

AK-47: Soviet-designed Kalashnikov automatic assault rifle widely used by military, terrorist, and insurgent forces around the world.

Alpha bombs: Rhodesian-made anti-personnel cluster bombs dropped from the Lynx ground support aircraft.

ASI: Air speed indicator.

ATC: Air traffic control.

ATPL: Airline transport pilot's licence.

BCR: Bronze Cross of Rhodesia, one rank below the Silver Cross of Rhodesia.

Bomb-shell: Terrorists would often split up, or 'bomb-shell' on initiation of a contact.

Braaivleis (Braai): Afrikaans word for a barbecue.

BSAP: British South Africa Police, Rhodesia's police force.

C of A: Certificate of airworthiness.

Callsign: A small unit of armed troops with its own radio identification.

Callup: Regular period of compulsory military and para-military service for white male civilians. By the end of the war, most men would spend six weeks in service and six weeks out.

Casevac: Casualty evacuation, mostly by air.

Chibuli: African word for beer.

Chilapalapa: African dialect combining simplified elements of other languages. (See also *Fanagalo*).

CO: Commanding Officer.

ComOps: Combined Operations Headquarters, Rhodesian Security Forces high command.

Contact: Armed engagement between Rhodesian Security Forces and terrorists.

CPL: Commercial pilot's licence.

Dagga: earth or termite mound mud used for building (also marijuana).

Dak: Douglas DC-3 all-purpose two-engine military and civilian aircraft.

Dambo: an area of marshy ground (See also *Vlei*).

DFC: Distinguished Flying Cross.

DZ: Drop zone. Designated landing zones for paratroops.

FAF: Forward airfield.

Fanagalo: dialect combining simplified elements of other languages (See also *Chilapalapa*).

Fireforce: Rhodesian-developed coordinated air-borne anti-terrorist troops and paratroops.

FN: Standard issue automatic assault rifle for the Rhodesian Security Forces, designed and manufactured by *Fabrique Nationale* of Belgium.

Frantan: Frangible napalm cannisters.

FRELIMO: *Frente de Libertação de Moçambique*, the socialist Mozambican regime whose armed forces of the same name provided military and political support to Rhodesian terrorists.

G-car: Alouette III helicopter gunship armed with twin .303 Browning machine guns.

GCV: Grand Cross of Valour, Rhodesian equivalent of the British Victoria Cross. Only two were awarded throughout the bush war.

Golf bombs: 200kg blast and shrapnel explosives deployed by the Lynx ground support aircraft.

GPU: Ground power unit.

Guti: African word for dense low cloud.

HALO: High altitude, low opening parachute technique used for covert cross-border operations.

IGS: Instrument guidance system.

ILS: Instrument landing system.

K-car: Kill-car or command-car, an Alouette III helicopter gunship armed with a MG 20mm canon, from which the army commander would direct operations on the ground.

Lemon: Unpromising or unsuccessful military operation.

Loc-stat: Military term for location status, generally based on a map reference or co-ordinates.

Lynx: Fixed-wing Reims-Cessna 337 Lynx, used as a ground assault and support aircraft. It carried twin .303 Browning machine guns and could deliver a combination of bombs, rockets, and napalm.

LZ: Landing zone for paratroops.

Mopani: African hardwood tree.

OC: Officer Commanding.

OCVR: Officer Commanding Volunteer Reserve.

OEO: Operations engineering officer.

OP: Observation post, usually on high ground.

Piccaninny kiah **(PK):** long-drop toilet.

Pitot tube: Device on a Dakota providing a pressure differential that feeds the altimeter.

PJI: Parachute jump instructor.

PPL: Private pilot's licence.

PTS: Parachute Training School.

RAR: Rhodesian African Rifles.

RhAF: Rhodesian Air Force.

RLI: Rhodesian Light Infantry.

Rondavel: Small round, thatched hut.

RPG: Rocket propelled grenade.

SAM-7: Russian-made Strela-2 shoulder-fired surface-to-air missile system.

SAS: Special Air Service. C Squadron SAS was the Rhodesian unit formed during the Malaysian crisis of the 1950s.

SB: Special Branch, a section of Rhodesia's British South Africa Police specialising in political intelligence.

SCR: Silver Cross of Rhodesia, one rank below the Grand Cross of Valour, and the equivalent to Britain's Distinguished Service Order.

Sky Shout: Pre-recorded anti-terrorist propaganda broadcast from low-flying aircraft.

SNEB rockets: 37mm air-to-ground rockets mounted under the wings of the Lynx air support aircraft.

SOP: Standard operating procedures.

Stick: A four-man unit of Rhodesian infantry, one carrying an MAG machine gun.

UANC: United African National Council, led by Bishop Abel Muzorewa.

VFR: Visual flight rules.

Vlei: An area of marshy ground (See also *Dambo*).

VNE: Never exceed speed for a DC-3 aircraft.

VR: Volunteer Reserve of the Rhodesian Air Force.

VSI: Vertical speed indicator.

ZANLA: Zimbabwe African National Liberation Army, headed by ZANU leader, Robert Mugabe.

ZANU: Zimbabwe African National Union, led by Robert Mugabe.

ZAPU: Zimbabwe African People's Union and its president, Joshua Nkomo.

ZIPRA: Zimbabwe People's Revolutionary Army, the military wing of ZAPU under the leadership of Joshua Nkomo.

Index

ATI 212

Atlantic 62, 112, 122, 149, 151

ATPL 82

ATR 215

Auschwitz 37

Australia 54

Avondale 78

Azores 123

B

Bader, Douglas 65

Baghdad, Iraq 123, 139, 145

Bahrain 134

Baldwin, Malcolm 'Baldy' 159

Ball, Albert 65

Banana, Reverend Canaan 190

Bangui, Central African Republic 144

Baragwanath Hospital 16

Barbour, David 109

Barcelona 176, 207

Barnett, Peter 126, 127

Basel, Switzerland 149

Basuto 23

Basutoland 23

Bay of Biscay 66

BBC 90

Beatrice 183

Beaumont, First Officer Garth 155

Beaver, Rich 203

Behrens, Heinz 37

Behrens, Scylla 37

Beira 87

Beit Bridge 183, 184

Belgian Congo 7, 55, 73, 74

C

Colombo 134

Coltishall 63

Combined Operations Headquarters (ComOps) 131, 157, 164, 177, 153, 180

Commercial pilot's licence (CPL)

Commonwealth 38, 56, 57, 185, 187

Commonwealth Day 38

ComOps 157, 164

Comoros Islands 76, 113, 115, 123, 148, 151, 155, 161, 164, 182, 210

Conditur in Petra 52

Congo 7, 55, 73, 74, 75, 100, 111, 123, 139, 152, 157

Cook, Vic 115

Copperbelt 25, 40

Corbishley, Peter 37

CPL 80

Cranwell 60, 64, 65, 66, 67, 68, 70, 118, 185

Croukamp, Dennis 144

Cuba 74, 149, 150, 193, 199

Cyprus 176

D

D'Hotman, Bob 114

Dakota (Dak) 80, 82, 96, 98, 106, 107, 114, 116, 117, 119, 131, 133, 137, 138, 140, 141, 143, 145, 146, 153, 154, 155, 158, 159, 160, 162, 163, 170, 176, 182, 183, 192, 200, 201, 214, 223, 230, 231, 233, 234, 236, 237

Damms, Air Vice Marshal Chris 108, 114

Daphne, David 38

Daphne, Peter 38

Daphne, Tony 38

Dar es Salaam 177

Dartmouth 68, 165

Darwendale dam 178

DC-3 Douglas Dakota 78, 80, 82, 83, 96, 98, 104, 106, 107, 109, 111, 156, 170, 214

DC-4 74, 81, 111

DC-7 (F) 100, 101, 109, 113, 156, 177, 179, 211, 214

DC-8 100, 101, 104, 111, 113, 121, 126, 133, 150, 152, 155, 156, 157, 160, 164, 165, 171, 172, 173, 174, 176, 183, 186, 189, 192, 193, 196, 197, 200, 203, 208, 211, 213, 214, 215, 217, 218

DCA 100, 101, 189, 213

D Day Normandy 226

De Goveia, Ken 37, 101, 172

de Havilland Chipmunk 65

de Ras, Adrian 102, 104

Deere, Alan 65

Deka River 92

Delhi 113

Delport, Mick 119

Democratic Republic of the Congo (DRC) 123, 152, 161, 193, 195, 213

Department of Civil Aviation 100

Dete 92

Dett 92

Dinard, Colonel Bob 74, 75, 76, 155, 164

Distinguished Flying Cross (DFC) 37

Dives, Dicky 79

Dixon, Squadron Leader Chris 158, 225

Djibouti 105

Domange, Jean-Louis 75, 111, 112

Donaldson, Ian 132

Doris 108, 109, 166, 183, 192

Douala, Cameroon 137

Douglas Aircraft Corporation 100

Douglas DC-3 78, 174

Dover 135

DRC 152, 161, 193, 195, 213

Dreaded, The 74

DSO 165

Duala, Cameroon 212

Dubai 123, 135, 161, 209

Dublin 201

Durban 181, 187, 207, 213

Durty Nelly's 104, 201

Dyer, George 104, 112, 115, 168, 188, 192

E

East Berlin 66

Edenvale 78

Eighth Army 37

England 19, 32, 41, 43, 61, 62, 63, 117, 168, 175

Esterhuizen, Elsie 155

F

FAF 84, 96, 114, 115, 146, 186, 224, 228, 230, 231, 232

Fairey, John 170, 182, 188

Falklands War 68

Farnborough 20

Fawkes, Guy 15

Federal Aviation Administration 202

Federation of Rhodesia and Nyasaland 54, 55

Fighter Command 20, 21

Fireforce 115, 116, 132, 135, 138, 153, 162, 227, 230

First World War 15, 17, 65

Fleche Noires 19

Fleming, John 168, 212

Flight 825 Air Rhodesia 155

Flight operations inspector (FOI) 78, 81

Forbes, Pat 137, 138

Fordson 36

Foreign Affairs Department 212

Forster, John 125, 147

Fort Victoria 118, 135, 142, 146

Forward air fields (FAFs) 84, 96, 146, 186

France 113, 148

Franceville 123

G

H

Johannesburg 16, 17, 19, 25, 31, 42, 104, 105, 117,121, 181, 186, 188, 189, 201, 207, 212, 213

Johnnie 210

Johnson, 'Johnnie' 65

Joint Operational Command/Centre (JOC) 96

Jorge do Limpopo 235

K

K-car 115, 116, 132, 162, 165, 167

Kabrit Barracks 227

Kai Tak airport 208

Kalashnikov 161

Kalomo 25, 28, 36, 37

Kamativi 57, 58, 60, 88, 92, 93, 144

Kamina 152, 153, 193, 196

Kano 105, 199, 207, 208, 215

Kariba 56, 60, 61, 73, 75, 96, 114, 155, 159, 167, 171, 178, 202, 222, 224, 228, 230

Kariba Breezes hotel 61

Katanga 74

Kaunda, Kenneth 90, 147

Kenya 55, 73

Keyter, Captain Chum 176

Khartoum 176, 181

Kigali 105

Kinnear, Henry 111

Kinshasa 75, 137, 172, 183, 193, 201

Kisangani 75

Kissinger, Henry 125, 148

KLM 32, 101, 102, 104, 133, 136, 189, 208, 215

Knightley, Phillip 12

Konsolas, Arnie 208

Korean War 97, 104, 176

Kriel, Neil 144

Kuwait 113, 123

L

M

M.A.S.H. 97

Maastricht 176

Mabalauta 107, 139, 140, 142

Machel, Samora 181

Madagascar 54

Madras 209

Madulo Pan 131, 132, 165

Maidenhead 63

Majorca 104, 120, 121, 133

Malan, 'Sailor' 65

Malan, DF 24

Malawi 54, 73, 211, 213

Malaysia 88

Mallett, Dave 126

Malloch, Captain Jack 'Boss' 74, 75, 76, 99, 100, 111, 112, 113, 126, 135, 145, 151, 152, 153, 155, 156, 164, 173, 176, 177, 182, 188, 189, 190, 191, 192, 193, 195, 199, 200, 204, 205, 211, 214, 220, 234

Malta 32, 37, 157, 171

Malvernia 112, 132, 139, 145

Mana Pools 97

Manchester 32

Mandir 195

Mann, Nori 214

Mannock, 'Mick' 65

Mapai 136

Maputo 69, 139, 160

Marandellas 41

Marondera 41

Marxist MPLA government 152

Marxist/Marxism 120, 152, 175, 191

Marymount Mission 137

Master Green rating 170, 211

Masvingo 118

O

P

Q

R

RAR 84, 120, 162

Red Arrows 19

Red One 159

Reid Daly, Lieutenant Colonel Ron 166, 187

Reid-Rowland, John 109

Reims 113, 116

Renault 4 80

RhAF 83, 111, 113, 114, 156, 165, 170, 174

Rheims 148

Rhodes University 59

Rhodes, Cecil 25, 53

Rhodesia 7, 11, 12, 19, 20, 23, 24, 25, 28, 33, 37, 38, 41, 42, 44, 46, 48, 51, 53, 54, 55, 56, 57, 58, 59, 60, 68, 73, 74, 75, 76, 77, 78, 80, 82, 83, 84, 87, 88, 89, 90, 96, 97, 99, 100, 101, 102, 107, 108, 109, 113, 115, 117, 118, 120, 125, 126, 131, 132, 133, 134, 136, 138, 144, 147, 148, 149, 155, 156, 157, 158, 159, 160, 161, 164, 165, 167, 168, 170, 171, 174, 175, 176, 177, 180, 181, 183, 184, 187, 188, 190, 212, 219, 221, 222, 223, 225, 226, 228, 230, 235

Rhodesia Broadcasting Corporation (RBC) 90, 136

Rhodesia Herald 156, 167

Rhodesian Light Infantry (RLI) 84, 117

Rhodesian African Rifles (RAR) 84, 120

Rhodesian Air Force (RhAF) 19, 76, 82, 83, 109, 156, 165, 221, 222, 223

Rhodesian Cold Storage Commission 161

Rhodesian Department of Civil Aviation (DCA) 100, 101, 78, 168, 189, 213

Rhodesian Front 174

Rhodesian Television (RTV) 97, 136

Ribble River 32

Richman, Sam 102, 103, 144, 161, 186, 189, 190, 218

RLI 107, 117, 131, 137, 223, 224, 226, 227, 228, 230, 232

Roberts, Skitch 193, 201, 212

Rock 32, 34

Rodwell, Aldwyn Horatio 15

Rodwell, Bruce (my father) 15, 16, 17, 19, 23, 29, 35, 36, 42, 43, 47, 48, 57, 58, 60, 61, 87, 88, 90, 91, 92, 93, 95, 183

T

U

UDI 52, 73, 188

UK 19, 51, 52, 58, 60, 62, 117, 136, 165, 168, 170, 188, 190, 192, 201

Umtali 51, 96, 112, 144, 190

Umtali Boys' High School 144

Umtata 187

Unilateral Declaration of Independence (UDI) 52, 59, 73

UNITA Angola 151, 152, 153, 191, 193, 200

United African National Council (UANC) 148

United Airlines 190

United Kingdom 16, 41, 54, 55, 87, 190

United Nations 87, 148, 168

United Nations Security Council 148

United Party 24

United States 74, 87, 146

University of Edinburgh 17

US 100, 151

US Federal Aviation Administration 202

USSR 87

V

V1 120

Van Wyk, Pete 20

VASI 152

VE Day 16

Venezuela 112, 123

Very cartridge 79

VFR 187, 213

Victoria Cross 65, 131

Victoria Falls 25, 31, 92, 148

Viscount 8, 102, 143, 145, 155, 157, 171, 175, 211, 222

Volunteer Reserve (VR) 82, 108, 230, 234

Vonhoff, Noel 97

W

Y

Z

Bibliography

The following publications proved helpful in producing this memoir:

Cole, Barbara: *The Elite. The Story of the Rhodesian Special Air Service*, Three Knights Publishing, Transkei 1984

Lovett, John: *Contact*, Galaxie Press, Salisbury, Rhodesia 1977

Moorcraft, Paul L: *Contact 2*, Sygma Books, Johannesburg 1981

Reid Daly, Lieutenant Colonel Ron, as told to Stiff, Peter: *Selous Scouts, Top Secret War*, Galago Publishing, Republic of South Africa, 1983

Salt, Beryl: *Pride of Eagles. A History of the Rhodesian Air Force*, Helion and Company, 2015

About the Author

Ian Rodwell has a lifelong career in aviation.

Born in Northern Rhodesia (Zambia) in 1949, he went to boarding school in Rhodesia (Zimbabwe). He graduated 18 months after Ian Smith announced the November 11 1965 Unilateral Declaration of Independence (UDI). UDI severed all links with Rhodesia's former colonial master, Great Britain. It also served as the catalyst to an increasingly violent 15-year black majority rule campaign, international pariah status, and a bloody bush war.

Rodwell trained as a cadet fighter pilot with the Royal Air Force from 1967 to 1969 before returning to Rhodesia.

Gaining first a private then a commercial aviation licence in Rhodesia, he progressed rapidly through a series of aviation sectors. He joined 3 Squadron (DC-3 Dakotas) of the Rhodesian Air Force (RhAF) in 1974. He continued his decorated flying career to the end of the war in 1980, working with airborne troops such as Rhodesia's crack Special Air Service, Selous Scouts, Rhodesian Light Infantry, and Rhodesian African Rifles in fireforce and cross-border missions. At the same time, he maintained a parallel career with Air Trans Africa/ Affretair, Rhodesia's famous under-cover, sanctions-busting air operation with the legendary Captain Jack Malloch.

The war over, he continued with Affretair till 1982 when, having qualified onto the Boeing 707, he joined the Saudi Arabian airline, Saudia, as a captain. He flew for Saudia for six years and then made the move to Cathay Pacific, based first in Hong Kong, then France. He was with Cathay Pacific for 26 years, rising to the rank of Chief Pilot of its worldwide Boeing 747 fleet.

He retired from flying in 2013 but continues to advise and consult on operations and training to aviation organisations around the world.

Rodwell and his wife, Trish, divide their time between homes and family in England and the south of France.